Colin McEvedy The Penguin Atlas of North American History

Maps devised by the author
and drawn by David Woodroffe

Penguin Books

INTRODUCTION

The subject of this Atlas is North America in general and the United States in particular. Its limits in time are 20,000 BC and AD 1870, i.e., it covers the period between the first appearance of *Homo sapiens* in this part of the world and the forcible reassertion, in the American Civil War, of the indissolubility of the Union. Since then the integrity of the continental United States has been unchallenged and its political outlines have undergone only minor changes. The story as told in this Atlas, which is essentially about how and why North America has acquired the boundaries that it has today, reaches its natural end with Grant's first administration.

A few additional points are perhaps worth making. The Atlas follows a format I have used before, with an unvarying base map on which the relevant archeological, political or demographic data are displayed. The text is a commentary on the maps, that is to say it is generated by changes in the data displayed, not conceived as a general history. There is, for example, a bit about Andrew Jackson's dealings with the British and the Indians but nothing about his campaign against the Bank of the United States. Similarly, although wars which changed the maps are given fair treatment, wars which did not, like the War of 1812, are dealt with summarily.

It seems hardly necessary to discuss the geographical limits chosen for the base map. Clearly a connected history of North America demands the inclusion of the Caribbean and as much of meso-America (Middle America, meaning Mexico and Central America) as possible: equally clearly, including Alaska and the Canadian north-west would unbalance the map to an absurd degree. The simplest defense of the map as finally drawn is that it covers 99 percent of the population and 99 percent of the action in the North American area in historical time.

It remains to be said that, by the standards of most historical atlases, this is a very small-scale map for a very big continent. It is no good trying to follow events in and around Boston in 1775 on maps of this type. On the other hand, it is surprising how looking at the wider picture sometimes enables one to understand why purely local events took the course they did. It is, for example, easier to understand what happened at Yorktown by studying a map that covers the whole theater of operations (which stretched from New York to the Caribbean) than by putting one's nose on a detailed map of the Yorktown Peninsula. In the case of the American Civil War, however, I have to admit that an important part of the narrative would be incomprehensible without some additional maps on a larger scale. So in this section I have contrived to have the best of both worlds by inserting in the text a set of nine maps showing the maneuverings that took place in the Virginian theater of operations. Even these, though, are intended to provide an overview, not a detailed tactical picture. They show the movements that led up to the battles, but not the battles themselves.

One aspect of American history that is not covered at all is the influence of America on the rest of the world. This matters less than one might think. In the pre-Columban era the effect was zero, while in the colonial period the American interests of the great powers of the time, though important in themselves, were always marginal to their essential concerns. And once the Thirteen Colonies of British North America and the mainland provinces of the Spanish–American Empire had gained their independence their affairs attracted even less debate in the councils of Europe. For much of the subsequent period – effectively for the whole span covered by the Atlas – the Old World and the New went their separate ways. There were, it is true, voices within the American Republic that called for an imperialist foreign policy even at this early date, but few paid much attention to them and the most striking instances of armed intervention outside the hemisphere were either trivial (like the bombardment of Tripoli in 1804) or essentially commercial (like the opening up of Japan by Commodore Perry in 1853–4). The empire Americans were looking for was not overseas but within their own geographical confines. The nation wholeheartedly agreed with John L. Sullivan when he wrote, 'It is our manifest destiny to overspread and possess the whole of the continent which Providence has given us.' And until that vision was consummated most Americans regarded the outside world as a distraction.

So this book is concerned with America's prehistory, its period of colonial tutelage and its heroic age, but not with its role in the world, nor even the first beginnings of this. That is another story for another time. This Atlas closes with hardly anyone aware that here was a country that would become, in the space of a few short years, the preoccupation, the wonder, and the envy of the world.

In drawing the maps that are the backbone of this book I have tried to present the essential facts of early-American history in a concise form. These days few facts go unchallenged and doubtless many of mine are less secure than I like to think. This must be true of the pre-Columban period where there are, strictly speaking, no facts at all, only interpretations of archeological and linguistic data. The best I can claim for this section of the Atlas is that it is not deliberately controversial. My aim has been to represent the current consensus.

This implies that a consensus exists. There is, however, one area where such a spirited attack has been mounted on the established view that it is difficult to know where orthodoxy currently resides – with the old or with the new, with the revolutionaries or with the defenders of the classical position. I refer to the conflicting schools of thought on early American demography.

The subject of this argument is purely quantitative. Were there 15 million people in the Americas on the eve of Columbus' voyage or were there several times this number? Specifically, were there a million Indians north of the Rio Grande or twice as many; were there 5 million people in Middle America or 10 million; were there 100,000 or 200,000 Arawak in Hispaniola? The answer has to be that we do not know and can never be sure. In the map that is concerned with the subject I have accepted the views of the classical school and opted for the lower set of figures. However, I would not deny that there is a case for doubling the value of the symbols used. It is just that I am not convinced by it.

If that is all there was to the controversy the dispute would hardly be worth the attention I am giving it here. It is, after all, obvious that figures for populations at this date must by hypothetical and could be multiplied by two without contradicting such evidence as there is. But what the hard-line revisionists have proposed is something of a quite different order: not 5 or 10 million in Middle America but 40 or 50, not 1 or 2 million in the area of the United States but 15 or 20, not one or two hundred thousand on Santo Domingo but – wait for it – more than 2 million. Faced with figures of this magnitude one is reminded of the story of the Duke of Wellington who, when a stranger came up to him and said, 'Mr Smith, I believe,' replied, 'Sir, if you can believe that, you can believe anything.'

Unfortunately it is not possible to make such a lordly dismissal in this case. The noble duke could, in the last analysis, document his title, but we have no census data for fifteenth-century America. We can only say that everything we know of nomadic and semi-agricultural peoples suggests that a population of 1 to 2 million for the area north of the Rio Grande would appear to be of the right order of magnitude and that when the first reasonably secure figures come in during the subsequent period they are consistent with a pre-Columban population of these dimensions. The high rollers, of course, claim that native numbers had been reduced to these low levels by epidemics of small-pox, measles and other diseases introduced from Europe – and indeed they could have been. But there is no record of any continental population being cut back by the sort of percentages needed to get from 20 million to 2 or 1 million. Even the Black Death reduced the population of Europe by only a third.

In truth, the whole idea of 20 million Indians in the continental USA is a fantasy, a poetic use of numbers to illustrate what is in essence an old literary favourite, the myth of the Golden Age. It is part of a vision of pre-Columban America as a simple and harmonious society where people were conceived without lust and lived without sin. It may be reasonable, at one level, to have a counter-vailing idea to set against the more ruthless view of the savage state as 'nasty, brutish and short' but no good can come of affronting common sense.

The instrument I would recommend to anyone looking at estimates of early populations is Occam's razor. Faced with the ever-thickening forests of theological speculation produced by medieval schoolmen, William of Occam enunciated the principle that has endeared him to logicians ever since. 'It is vain to do with more what can be done with less,' he said, and proceeded to strike out all theories that were not actually needed to explain ascertainable facts. Although he did not mean quite what I want him to mean, there is a lot to be said for applying his words literally to early population estimates. Historical demography is a field in which the minimum makes the best maximum.

Atlases of this class – one hesitates to call them popular in case they turn out not to be so – are compilations, dependent on other people's researches and inspiration. It would be tedious to enumerate the sources I have used and, as they are to be found in any standard history, I have refrained from doing so. I must, however, acknowledge the support I have received from my publishers, both Viking in the United States and Penguin in the United Kingdom, from my secretary, Sandra Cook, and from my wife and children. Particularly the latter without whom, to quote P. G. Wodehouse, this book would have been finished in half the time.

3

During the last 2 million years or so – the period geologists call the Pleistocene – the earth's climate has been unstable, alternating between phases of extreme cold (Ice Ages or Glacials) and phases when the average temperatures were comparable to today's (Interglacials). Quite why this happened no one knows. There are fluctuations in the amount of sunlight that the earth receives but they are small and, even if they can explain the timing of individual peaks and troughs in the climatic record (which is doubtful), they are of no help in determining why the instability arose in the first place. Most likely it is something to do with the changes that have taken place in the configuration of the continents. These continental movements are slow but can have relatively sharp cut-offs. For example, the closing of the gap between North and South America, something that is known to have happened at about the time the Pleistocene began, must have caused a major redistribution of oceanic currents and done so quite abruptly. Indeed, it is quite possible that this is the trigger we are looking for. By substituting longitudinal weather cells for latitudinal ones it could well have been responsible for creating the Pleistocene pattern of climate with its built-in 'flip-flop' instability.

Be that as it may, there is no doubt about the state of North America at the height of the last Ice Age. The whole of Canada (97 percent, to be exact) and a notable part of the northern United States (the Great Lakes region, New England and much else besides) was buried under a sheet of ice that averaged a mile in depth and in places reached twice that. So immense was the quantity of water locked up in this and similar ice-caps elsewhere in the world that the sea-level was lowered by 100 meters. As a result, the map of America which begins our series is fattened out by comparison with today's, with chunkier peninsulas and narrowed seas. The west coast does not look all at that different because the coastal ranges drop sharply into the Pacific Ocean and 100 meters vertically does not make much difference to the shape of the shore. However, the gently shelving eastern seaboard is completely recast: the Atlantic lies fifty miles or more further out than at present and takes a much simpler line.

The Pacific coast is steep because it is the advancing edge of the continent. For 100 million years now North America has been moving westward, a movement that has created the parallel mountain ridges, the *cordilleras*, that are characteristic of the western United States and Mexico. The process of mountain building is not quite as simple as this makes it sound – there is more to it than just a crumpling effect – but this is the essence of it and all mountain chains are now thought to have their origins in movements of this type. The Appalachians of the eastern United States, for example, are ascribed to an earlier period when America was drifting the other way and banging up against the Old World. On this interpretation the eastern seaboard represents some Atlantic detritus that came away with America when the two continents finally parted company, while Florida has its origins in the encounter with Africa that occurred at the same time.

The Appalachians in the east and the *cordilleras* in the west determined the drainage of the great ice-cap; it could only be due south, into the Gulf of Mexico. So the continent's main river system – the Missouri–Mississippi–Ohio complex – was basically the same as it is today. So were the closed systems, the Nevada and Utah basins, though, because the cold had reduced the evaporation rate, the lakes at the bottom of them, known to geologists as Lakes Lahontan and Bonneville, were larger than their equivalents today. Lake Missoula, in western Montana, illustrates another class of lake that was important in the glacial era. Fed by meltwater from the ice-cap that at the same time blocked its natural drainage, it depended on the ice-cap retaining its local geography. When, shortly after the date of this map, the glaciers began to retreat, the waters the ice had dammed back emptied into the Columbia and Lake Missoula ceased to exist.

As for the animals that ranged Ice-Age America, they were a more varied lot than those existing today. A selection of them was mired in the tar pits of Rancho La Brea, in the heart of present-day Los Angeles and their well-preserved remains can be seen within a few yards of Wilshire Boulevard. This 'Rancholabrean fauna' includes mammoth and mastodon, horses, camels and giant bison, together with the animals that preyed on them, saber-tooths, wolves, mountain lions and coyotes. In addition to these long-time residents of North America, there are some species that had moved up from South America via the newly established isthmus; some familiar to us, like the armadillo and opossum, others, like the lumbering 'ground sloths', more exotic. One important species that is missing is man. Despite many claims to the contrary, it is clear that at the time of the Wisconsin glaciation – the geologists' term for the ice-cap at its final maximum – no human being had ever set foot in North America. The ice formed too great a barrier to cross.

So, no one was in Arizona to witness the last major physical interaction between the earth and the cosmos, the impact of the Barringer meteor at around the date of this map. A kilometer-sized nickel-iron object weighing anything up to a quarter of a million tons, it gouged out a circular crater 170 meters (570 feet) deep and 1,240 meters (4,100 feet) across. The relatively recent date means that its outline is still crisp: the sight is as near to a visit to the moon as most of us are likely to get.

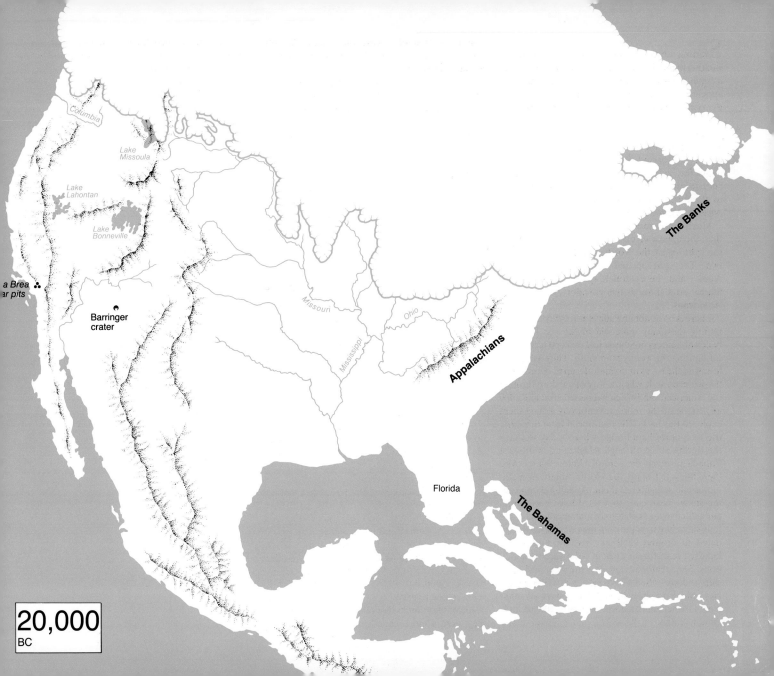

Columbia

Lake
Missoula

Lake
Lahontan

Lake
Bonneville

a Brea
ar pits

Barringer
crater

Missouri

Ohio

Mississippi

Appalachians

The Banks

Florida

The Bahamas

20,000
BC

Starting about 16,000 years ago the world's weather began to improve. The North American ice-gap got smaller: as it shrank meltwater lakes appeared along its margin and gradually assumed the outline we associate with the Great Lakes. In their original forms the Great Lakes tended to be bigger than their present-day descendants because the weight of the ice-cap had depressed the area where they formed. However, none of them could match the vast Lake Agassiz of central Canada, the ancestor of Lake Winnipeg. With its natural outlet to the north still dammed by the ice-cap, Lake Agassiz became a veritable inland sea.

Much more important from our point of view than the appearance of these bodies of water was the splitting of the North American ice-cap into two. The split opened up a corridor between Alaska and the central lowlands of the United States. And through this corridor came the first Americans.

There is no doubt nowadays as to who they were. During the many millennia of the last Ice Age, bands of hunters in Siberia had evolved techniques for hunting the woolly mammoth. They habitually followed the herds of mammoths up to the edges of the ice-caps and, when a way opened up through the American cap (which happened around 10,000 BC), some of the more adventurous among them explored this path. They advanced from Beringia, the temporary land-bridge where today we have the Bering Strait, through Alaska and north-west Canada to reach the central United States. And there they fell upon the North American mammoths and slaughtered them. At half a dozen sites the stone spearheads they used have been found embedded in the skeletons of mammoths and at the four sites shown on the map the remains have been dated to around 9250 BC, give or take a few hundred years for the error in radio-carbon estimations. The spearheads are all of the same workmanship and are called Clovis points after the site in New Mexico where their priority over all other North American artifacts was first convincingly demonstrated.

The newcomers were probably very few in number. A single band of thirty to sixty individuals could well have multiplied into 500 bands and a total population of 10,000 within five centuries. This would be enough to provide a scattering of people across the whole of the United States and Mexico. It is also about the right rate of growth both geographically and demographically and it fits with the archeological and paleontological data. Clovis points have been found across the entire United States just as mammoth bones of the right date occur throughout North America and Mexico.

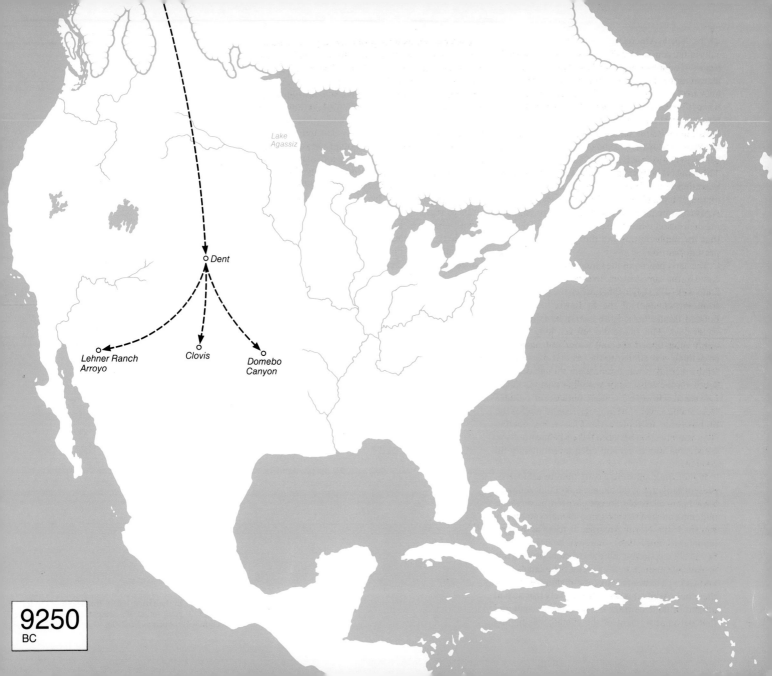

Lake Agassiz

Dent

Lehner Ranch Arroyo

Clovis

Domebo Canyon

9250
BC

The North American ice-caps shrank dramatically in the course of the eighth and seventh millennia BC. The western (Cordilleran) cap dwindled to almost nothing, the eastern (Laurentide) cap drew back to the north, split into two and let the sea into what is now Hudson Bay. Lake Agassiz was now able to use its natural line of drainage, the Nelson River, and became smaller as a result. By contrast the Hudson Bay of the time (the Tyrrell Sea of the geologists) was much bigger than today's version. This was because the earth's crust in the region had been depressed by the weight of the ice-cap and, although it had begun to return to normal, the recovery process was very sluggish. This continuing depression more than counterbalanced the fact that the sea-level was still thirty meters below its present position.

The early history of the Great Lakes was complicated by the same factors. In their original form the lakes were so low-lying that, when the ice withdrew from the channel of the St Lawrence, the sea flooded in and turned the nearer lakes into salt-water bays. This phase did not last long. Crustal uplift soon tipped the salt water out again and something very similar to the present-day chain of freshwater lakes was established, though draining south via the Mississippi as well as east via the St Lawrence. However, neither outlets nor outlines were stable as yet. The long-term trend was for the St Lawrence to replace the Mississippi, but the Illinois connection between Lake Michigan and the Mississippi was to remain open intermittently till 2000 BC.[1]

If the continent took a long time to achieve its present geography, the change in its fauna seems to have been relatively abrupt. Within a couple of millennia most of the big-game animals completely vanished: the North America of 6500 BC had no mammoths, mastodons, camels or horses. Man has been held responsible for these extinctions and this is plausible enough in the case of the animals he is known to have hunted, like the mammoth. As for the others, while it is not at all unlikely that he had a hand in their demise, it has to be remembered that the improvement of the climate was tipping the ecological balance against large animals. One of their main advantages is that they conserve heat better than small ones, and this benefit became less important as the weather moderated.

Declining though the bigger animals might be, there were still enough buffalo of various types (including *Bison occidentalis*, half as big again as the bison of today) to keep the paleo-Indians of the plains well fed. But what of other areas? Archeologists contrast the characteristic tool of the buffalo hunters, the large flint spearpoint, with the smaller flint points found in the western and eastern parts of the United States. This suggests that the hunters in these regions had turned to smaller game. And from what we know of comparable cultures elsewhere, it seems certain that they were supplementing their diet by general foraging, by the collection of nuts, berries and seeds. Indeed, in the desert areas of the south-west USA we know that such items soon became the staple and game the supplement.

1 The uplift in the Great Lakes area continues to this day and if it goes on at its present rate the Illinois connection will reopen in AD 3500.

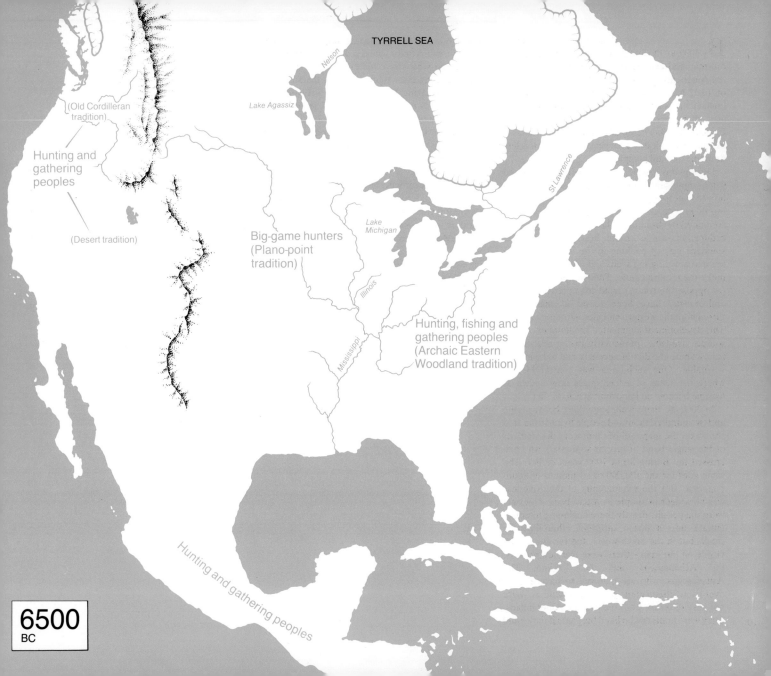

TYRRELL SEA

Nelson

Lake Agassiz

St Lawrence

(Old Cordilleran
tradition)

Hunting and
gathering
peoples

(Desert tradition)

Lake
Michigan

Big-game hunters
(Plano-point
tradition)

Illinois

Mississippi

Hunting, fishing and
gathering peoples
(Archaic Eastern
Woodland tradition)

Hunting and gathering peoples

6500
BC

By 3000 BC the last ice had gone from the area of our map and the sea had risen to its present level: the American continent finally assumed its familiar outline. Along the east coast the flooding of the lowlands produced the convoluted coastlines that are characteristic of drowned river valleys, Chesapeake Bay being about as good an example as you could ask for. Elsewhere the effect was less dramatic but still complicating.

During this period the paleo-Indians evolved some significant new techniques. They learned how to waterproof the baskets they wove, by caulking them with clay, and how to boil the water so contained by dropping in heated stones. This procedure, known as 'stone boiling', became the standard way of cooking in the west. They also learned how to grind seeds and nuts into a paste to make them more edible. Their simple, in-and-out (as opposed to rotary) grindstone pairs, the *mano* and *metate*, have been found at many sites throughout the western and meso-American areas. This development augmented the number of food sources available, particularly in the near-desert zones where the diet of necessity had to be mainly vegetable. One such area was central Mexico where the seeds of a local grass now known as *teosinte* became an important article of diet.

In 3000 BC there were something between one and two hundred thousand people living in the area shown on the map. All of them were descendants of the single band of fifty or so hunters who had crossed the Bering Strait 7000 years earlier. The same goes for the 100,000 or so Indians of South America. But the ethnography of the Americas was no longer as simple as it had been. Not only were the people already there beginning to differentiate into a dozen different ethno-linguistic stocks but in the north-west – too far away to be visible on our map – there were two new arrivals, the Athapascans and the Eskimo. The Athapascans, who are believed to have crossed over from Siberia in the sixth millennium BC, were not very different from the original Amerindians. They were hunters who liked big game if they could get it and, in the caribou and moose of the Canadian sub-Arctic, found a fair amount of it. The Eskimo who arrived later, around 4000 BC, were something else. While living on the Siberian side of the Bering Strait they had evolved the equipment they needed to make a success of seal- and walrus-hunting, and these aquatic mammals, together with salmon, remained their main source of food when they moved to America. This meant that their distribution was to be restricted to the northern coastline. Neither now nor later did they have much contact with any of the peoples of the interior.

A major volcanic event which belongs in this period is the massive eruption that destroyed Mount Mazama in the Oregon sector of the Cascades in approximately 4650 BC. The explosion, which had ten times the force of the Mount St Helens eruption of 1980, blew the mountain apart, creating the central void now occupied by Crater Lake. The result is the deepest and, many would say, the most beautiful body of fresh water in the United States.

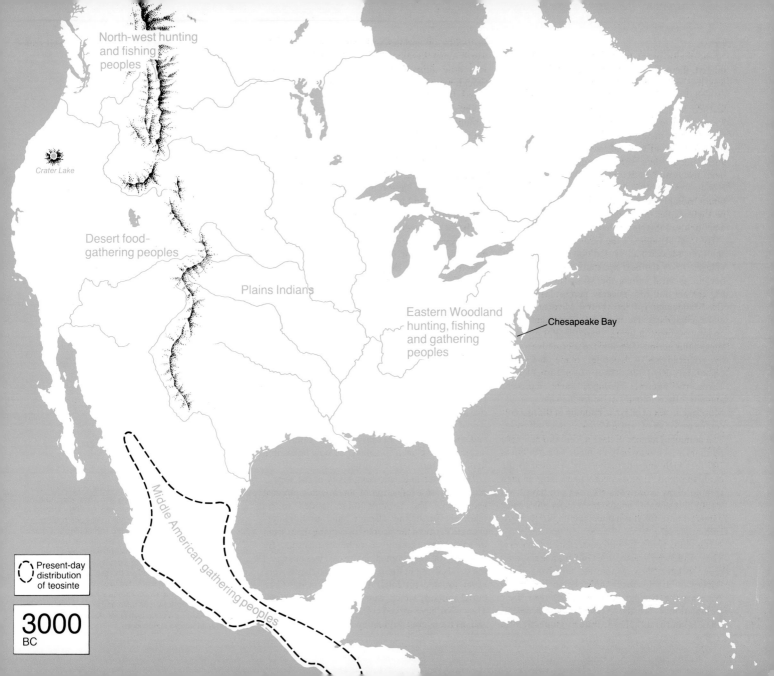

North-west hunting
and fishing
peoples

Crater Lake

Desert food-
gathering peoples

Plains Indians

Eastern Woodland
hunting, fishing
and gathering
peoples

Chesapeake Bay

Middle American gathering peoples

Present-day
distribution
of teosinte

3000
BC

The major event between 3000 and 500 BC – indeed, the major event of American prehistory – was the appearance of farming communities in central Mexico. The people there had already learned how to harvest *teosinte* seed. Now they learned how to cultivate the plant and, in doing so, how to select the most suitable strains for replanting. A thousand years of this produced maize, a variety of *teosinte* with a greatly enlarged seed-bearing cob and seeds that are much easier to mill. Besides maize the Mexicans cultivated other plants, notably beans and squash, but maize was to be their staple: the fields of the American Indian were fields of this 'Indian corn'.

By 1500 BC some of the farmers of central and southern Mexico had settled down in permanent villages. Over the next ten centuries such villages became general among the Maya (the people of Guatemala and the Yucatan peninsula) and the Oto-Mangueans (of the central Mexican valleys and Pacific coast). The new lifestyle brought with it an improvement in living standards. Pottery from sites of this period – labelled the 'Formative' phase by archeologists – is better made and more elaborately decorated than any from earlier levels. Terracotta figurines abound: some represent animals, others humans or, more than likely, gods. Most significant of all is the building of the first cult center we know of, at La Venta on the Gulf coast. The dominant feature of the La Venta complex is a pyramid which may only be made of earth but is 100 feet high and approximately oriented to the cardinal points. It looks over a plaza large enough to hold many more villagers than can have lived locally. Presumably people from many miles away gathered here for ceremonies relating to the agricultural cycle.

It is unlikely that La Venta is a chance discovery. The people who lived on the Gulf coast at this time seem to have been responsible for giving meso-American architecture and religion (in meso-America the two go hand in hand) their basic formulation. It is usual to refer to these people as Olmecs, and as such they feature prominently in all textbooks of middle-American prehistory. It is worth remembering, however, that we really have very little direct information on them, and that though we call them Olmecs we have no idea what they called themselves.[1]

The northern third of Mexico is less suitable for farming than the center and south and though the people who lived there, the Uto-Aztecs, did grow maize, their way of life is best characterized as semi-agricultural; they still depended on hunting and gathering for a major part of their food supply. This meant that they remained at least intermittently mobile and it is possible that some of them were already drifting northward across the present-day border between Mexico and the United States. If so, they will have been the first food-producers to enter the area, for all the peoples native to that region were still at the food-gathering stage.

These native North Americans can be divided into three linguistic groups. The area east of the Rockies belonged to the macro-Algonkian stock, Algonkian proper being spoken in the eastern Woodland zone, languages of the Siouan sub-group on the plains between the Rockies and the Mississippi. Algonkian speakers also ranged the whole of southern Canada from Pacific to Atlantic. The other two linguistic stocks, Penutian and Hokan, were confined to the relatively less extensive area south of Canada and west of the Rockies. And if there is a case to be made for a fourth stock, and there could be because not all Amerindian languages have been classified, it would be located in this area too.

The greater linguistic complexity in the west is probably just a reflection of the region's physical geography. The habitats there tended to be relatively small and discrete, and useful interchanges between the peoples occupying them seem to have been exceptional rather than usual. By contrast, the environment in the east was open and the bands living in the plains and woodlands were never isolated for long. This shows in the large burial mounds which were erected at this time. They must have served considerable communities and, as the overall population density was still very low, this means that they must have served considerable areas.

1 The name Olmec is taken from the people who lived in this area in the fifteenth century AD. They were relatives of the Aztecs and like them had only recently arrived in central Mexico; no way could they have been responsible for La Venta. Who was – who the archeologists' Olmecs were – is something about which no one can be sure, but the easiest way of making sense of the present-day distribution of Mayan-speaking peoples is to assume that they were Mayan. This bridges the gap between the main Mayan group in Yucatan and its Huastec outlier further up the Gulf. Perhaps the word Tamoanchan fits in here. An Aztec legend mentions it as the name of a famous people, or perhaps site (La Venta itself?), on the 'Eastern Sea' and it is a Mayan not an Aztec word.

PENUTIAN

and

HOKAN

groups

MACRO-

ALGONKIAN

developing
SIOUAN sub-stock

STOCK

UTO-AZTECS

farming
zone

OTO-MANGUEANS

HUASTECS

La Venta

OLMECS

MAYA

500
BC

The construction of a calendar is one of the most important intellectual challenges facing an agricultural people. The meso-Americans rose to it splendidly, inventing a set of signs (known as glyphs) and a system of numerals (a dot for one, a bar for five) which enabled them to record both the day of the month and the date of the year. The year dates were calculated from a base-line equivalent to 3113 BC when the Middle Americans reckoned that the world as we know it had been created. The two earliest examples found so far are from Chiapa de Corzo (an inscription of 36 BC) and Tres Zapotes (31 BC). Tres Zapotes was the main Olmec ceremonial center at this time (La Venta had been abandoned around 400 BC) and Chiapo de Corzo was in the area of Olmec influence. This makes it more than likely that the meso-Americans owe their calendar, like so many other things, to this mysterious people.

If, as the meso-Americans often did, you identify individuals by their birth dates, a calendar gets you more than half-way towards inscriptions which have some history in them. For example, the Mexican equivalent of the biblical 'David smote Goliath' would be '2 July smote 8 August'. All that a Mexican needed to write this down was a glyph for 'smote'. At Monte Alban, the ceremonial center of the Zapotec Indians, there is a set of glyphs that look very much as if they are being used in this way. They suggest that the Middle-American area was on the verge of literacy by the beginning of the Christian era.

Monte Alban is a dramatic site, built on a hilltop overlooking the Oaxaca Valley. The slopes are dotted with the tombs of Zapotec nobles. At the top is a ceremonial plaza with a dozen buildings of various shapes and sizes ranged round it. One of them, building L, is remarkable for a set of carvings of 'dancers' who are clearly in their death throes, if not dead already. Although the guides will tell you that these are priests in a state of ecstasy (or alternatively that building L was a medical center and that the 'dancers' had come there for treatment) there is no doubt at all that these are sacrificial victims and that human sacrifice was already established as the central rite in meso-American religious ceremonial. This sacrificial religion was to form the basis for the achievements of the next, Classic, phase of meso-American civilization which is conventionally dated to the period AD 300–900.

Note that maize-growing communities were now established in the south-west of the United States, specifically in the Mogollon Hills of Arizona, a development that marks the beginning of agriculture in this region. Another culture making its first appearance on this map is the original version of the Eskimo tradition. From their original focus around the Bering Strait, the proto-Eskimo spread in two directions, south and east. The southern branch developed into the Aleut group of peoples which became the dominant stock of Alaska and the Aleutian Islands. None of them came far enough south to show up on our map. The eastern branch, the Eskimo proper, spread across the Arctic coastline of Canada, eventually reaching Greenland. Most of them, like the Aleuts, remain outside our field of view, but a few bands diverted southwards along the Atlantic coast and are visible on this map in Ungava and Labrador. At this stage in their development they lacked some of the items we consider characteristic of the Eskimo lifestyle. They had sleds but not dogs, for example, and they were not as yet ready to go after whale. Still, in their dependence on seal and salmon they already displayed the essential elements of this Arctic culture.

The Classic phase of meso-American prehistory (for which see the next map, dated AD 500) is associated in most people's minds with the Maya. This is not unreasonable, for Mayan sites of this period are the show-pieces of Middle American civilization. The buildings have a grandeur and the bas-reliefs that decorate them an elegance that cannot be matched elsewhere. The inscriptions too are in a class of their own. The dating formulas are accompanied by long series of glyphs which, though we cannot be sure of the meaning of more than the odd one here and there, clearly give more information about who was smiting whom than ever before.

Nevertheless, in one respect the Maya were not so advanced as the Mexicans to the north. Most of the Maya lived in homesteads scattered across the countryside, only a few lived in villages and nowhere in the Mayan zone was there anything resembling a town. But the Mexicans (meaning the inhabitants of the Mexico Valley) typically lived in villages, some of them of considerable size, and their main ceremonial center, Teotihuacan, had grown into something that has to be called a town. Covering several square miles, it must have had a population of at least 20,000, which makes it unique as far as the New World is concerned and a considerable place even by Old World standards. In contemporary Europe, for example, only Constantinople and Rome were bigger; places like London and Paris were a great deal smaller.

However, having said this, one has to add that in some important ways Teotihuacan was not a town at all, just an overgrown village. The essence of urbanization is specialization. Townsfolk produce a wide range of goods and services and, by marketing these, they obtain the products of the countryside: in both a physical and financial sense they are importers of food. All the available evidence suggests that there was nothing like this going on in Teotihuacan or, for that matter, in later meso-American 'cities' like Tenochtitlan. Their populations consisted almost entirely of peasant farmers who raised corn on garden-sized plots attached to their homes. The skills at their disposal were no greater than those of the surrounding countryfolk. What was unusual about Teotihuacan was its scale, not its style.

If scale is the only distinguishing feature of the Middle American 'city', the reasons it appeared when and where it did are not far to seek. The key is the lake that occupied the center of the Mexico Valley. Its salt contaminated the nearby fields and the only way the local farmers could cope with the problem was to flush the salt out with fresh water

UNGAVA

ESKIMO

LABRADOR

Northwest hunting and fishing peoples

Desert food gathering peoples

Plains hunters

Mogollon maize farmers

Eastern Woodland hunting, fishing and gathering peoples

Teotihuacan △

Cuicuilco △   △ Cholula

Dzibichaltun △

△ Yaxuna

Tres Zapotes △

Monte Alban △

△ Uaxactun

Chiapa de Corzo △

△ △ Tikal

Altar de Sacrificios

Izapa △

El Baul △ △ Kaminaljuyu

AD 1

from the springs in the surrounding hills. In doing so they discovered the potential of irrigating agriculture and obtained a dramatic increase in yields. This in turn supported an increase in population that was expressed both as a rise in total numbers and as an increase in settlement size. This sequence of events gave Middle America its first 'city'. Of greater importance, it conferred on the Mexico Valley the dominating position in Middle American demography which it has retained ever since.

The dominance was quickly reflected in the political sphere. There are bas-reliefs at Monte Alban which show the Zapotec nobility formally greeting a delegation from Teotihuacan. The fact that this meeting was recorded at all suggests an act of submission on the part of the Zapotec. Signs of Mexican influence are also to be found on the Gulf coast, particularly at the Totonac center of El Tajin and at the Olmec site of Cerro de las Mesas. Altogether, it seems more than likely that the rulers of Teotihuacan had established some form of empire over the central Mexican area.

What is not likely is that this Mexican Empire stretched into Guatemala – campaigning over distances of this magnitude was to prove beyond even the Aztec armies – so it comes as a surprise to find that the site that duplicates Teotihuacan's architecture most exactly is Kaminaljuyu, the Mayan center in the Guatemalan highlands. The explanation is probably to be found in the migration of the Pipil, a Mexican clan that is known to have moved south at around this time. If so, the Pipil must have arrived in Guatemala as a conquering elite and the hegemony over the southern half of the country that the construction of Kaminaljuyu implies is likely to have lasted throughout the Classic period.[1]

In North America, farming was now an established practice not only in the south-west but in the Mississippi valley as well. Exactly how farming techniques got from the Rio Grande to the Mississippi is unknown. It is unlikely to have been by sea because the much smaller gap between Yucatan and Cuba proved to be more than Middle American sailors could manage, while western and central Texas seem too barren to have supported farming communities of even the most transient sort. Most probably the pathway was littoral. A few semi-agricultural bands drifting along the Gulf coast could well have done the job.

The culture that evolved in the Mississippi Valley spread through the entire area. Its best-known artifacts are its earthworks and the state that has the most, the most varied and the most impressive of these, is Ohio. Besides the communal burial mounds that are the hallmark of the culture, there are banks outlining circular, square or polygonal enclosures, others that run in parallel for literally miles and some that are laid out in the shape of animals – the most famous being the Serpent Mound, near Cincinnati, which is a quarter of a mile long. The system of beliefs that these works imply is referred to by archeologists as the Hopewell cult. It remained the dominant ideology in the eastern Woodland zone until the eighth century AD.

By the date of this map the first farmers had arrived in the Caribbean islands. The people concerned, the Arawak, were natives of Venezuela. They moved into the Lesser Antilles around AD 100 and made such rapid progress through the island chain that they reached Puerto Rico within 100 years. The Lesser Antilles south of the Virgin Islands had previously been uninhabited but there were some simple gathering folk – the archeologists refer to them as the Ciboney – living in the Greater Antilles and Virgin Islands. They had been there for at least a thousand years, probably coming originally from Florida via the Bahamas.

In Newfoundland the Eskimo established a seasonal camp at the site now known as Port aux Choix, from which they preyed on the seals passing through the Strait of Belle Isle. This was as far south as the Eskimo were to get.

1 The sites marked in meso-America are the ones that are believed to have been the centers of major chieftainships. Not shown are some archeologically famous ones such as Quirigua and Bonampak which are thought to have been subordinate to more powerful neighbors (Copan and Yaxchilan respectively in the case of these two).

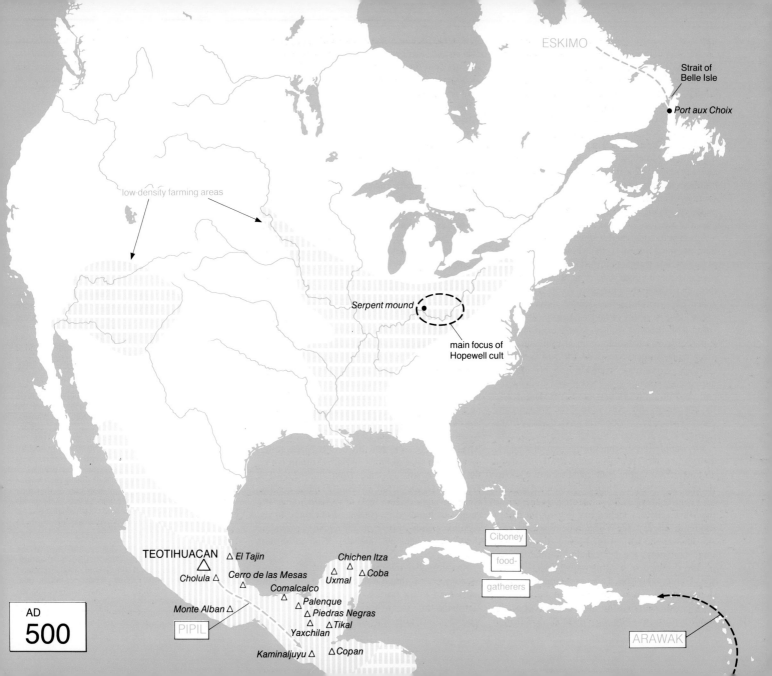

ESKIMO

Strait of
Belle Isle

● Port aux Choix

low-density farming areas

Serpent mound ●

main focus of
Hopewell cult

TEOTIHUACAN
△ El Tajin
Chichen Itza
Cholula △
△
Cerro de las Mesas
△ Coba
△
Uxmal
Comalcalco
△
△ Palenque
Monte Alban △
△ Piedras Negras
△
△ Tikal
Yaxchilan
Kaminaljuyu △
△ Copan

Ciboney

food-

gatherers

ARAWAK

PIPIL

AD
500

The dominance of Teotihuacan came to an abrupt end in the seventh century when the city was abandoned and the great works on which its inhabitants had labored so long were left to crumble. Over the next 200 years signs of the same neglect appear at one after another of the ceremonial centers in meso-America. Most of these had never had much in the way of permanent population, but they had been in regular use as meeting places. Now the sites went unvisited, their buildings fell into ruin and the jungle swallowed up some of them altogether. By AD 900 the Classic phase of Middle American civilization was over: even the memory of it was beginning to fade.

It is easy to make all this sound more mysterious than it was. Societies that build mounds and pyramids, and a great many pre- and proto-historic societies have done so, characteristically go through periods when they give up the whole idea. After all, pyramid cities are of only marginal utility. If it is useful to know when to plant your crops, a bit of advice from an experienced neighbor is probably as much help as an official announcement from Stonehenge. And the sun comes up whether you sacrifice virgins to it or not. But the impulse to worship usually reasserts itself in the end, and in tenth-century meso-America, just as the last centers still active were about to give up the ghost, a new wave of ritualism was unleashed in the north.

The people responsible for this revival were the Toltecs of Tula. They ran a more tightly organized and more thoroughly militarized society than any that had gone before. Their rule extended not only over central Mexico but, via an offshoot that seized the Mayan city of Chichen Itza towards the end of the tenth century, the Yucatan peninsula as well. As this was the part of the Mayan zone that was important now, the central and southern areas having declined into comparative insignificance, the Toltecs and the Toltec religion effectively dominated all of meso-America that mattered.[1]

In North America the important event of the tenth century was the movement of Athapascan bands into the south-west. For the farming peoples this meant the end of the good life. Whatever differences there were between the various Athapascan groups, the locals had only one word for the lot of them, *apache*, meaning 'enemy'. The Paiute of southern Utah suffered so badly from Apache harassment that they gave up trying to keep their farms going and drifted back into food gathering. Elsewhere the farmers sought security in numbers, abandoning their isolated homesteads in favor of communal villages, the famous *pueblos* of the south-west. The biggest of these pueblos, some of them capable of holding a thousand or more people, are marked on the map. Apart from Taos, the names are all modern and, of course, the Aztecs of Mexico had nothing to do with the pueblo in New Mexico imaginatively named after them.[2]

At about the date of this map Europeans paid their first visit to America. The explorers were Norse, from the settlements established on Greenland a generation earlier. After reconnoitering the coast of Labrador, which they called Markland, they attempted to plant a colony in 'Vinland' (probably Newfoundland). Dismayed by the wilderness they faced and discomfited by the hostility of the natives they encountered, they gave up and went home after a period that certainly was no longer than two or three years. Some archeologists believe that excavations at a site in northern Newfoundland known as L'Anse aux Meadows have uncovered the remains of this Norse settlement; others are dubious. What is certain is that the venture was doomed from the start. The Greenland colony itself was barely viable, needing constant support from Iceland to keep going. The couple of hundred Norse who lived there in the eleventh century were quite incapable of providing the sort of back-up that the Vinland settlers needed.

An alternative interpretation of the L'Anse aux Meadows site is that it was an Eskimo camp of the same kind as the earlier one at Port aux Choix. Certainly this was a busy time for the Eskimo whose culture now appears in its fully developed form, complete with husky dogs and whaling boats. The advances in technique can reasonably be attributed to the Inuit, an aggressive clan which succeeded in imposing itself and its lifestyle on all the Eskimo bands in the region.[3]

1 One of the best publicized meso-American legends concerns the Toltec hero, Quetzalcoatl, who founded Tula, was tricked into leaving it, conquered Chichen and then sailed away across the sea into the sunrise. It seems unlikely that there was ever any such person; he would have to have lived a very long time to have both founded Tula and conquered Chichen. Probably the story is just a way of crediting these achievements to the God of the same name who had long been a Mexican favorite.

2 Archeologists follow the Apache in applying the term Anasazi, meaning 'ancient ones', to the builders of the pueblos in southern Colorado and northern New Mexico. They use a different term, Hohokam, for the culture centered on Casa Grande. It is generally accepted that the Anasazi are the ancestors of the present-day Hopi pueblo-dwellers and that the Hohokam people are represented today by the Pima.

Exactly what route the Apache took during their migration is anyone's guess; the suggestion here is that they reached the south-west via the plains. A subsidiary movement which may or may not have occurred at the same time was to take a few bands of Athapascans into northern California.

3 For the archeologist this change is marked by the replacement of the Dorset culture by the Thule culture, the type-sites being in Baffin Island and Greenland respectively. The word Eskimo is an Algonkian one, meaning 'eaters of raw flesh'. It can reasonably be applied to the Arctic community throughout its history, which allows us to reserve the term Inuit for its final phase. All present-day Eskimo refer to themselves as Inuit.

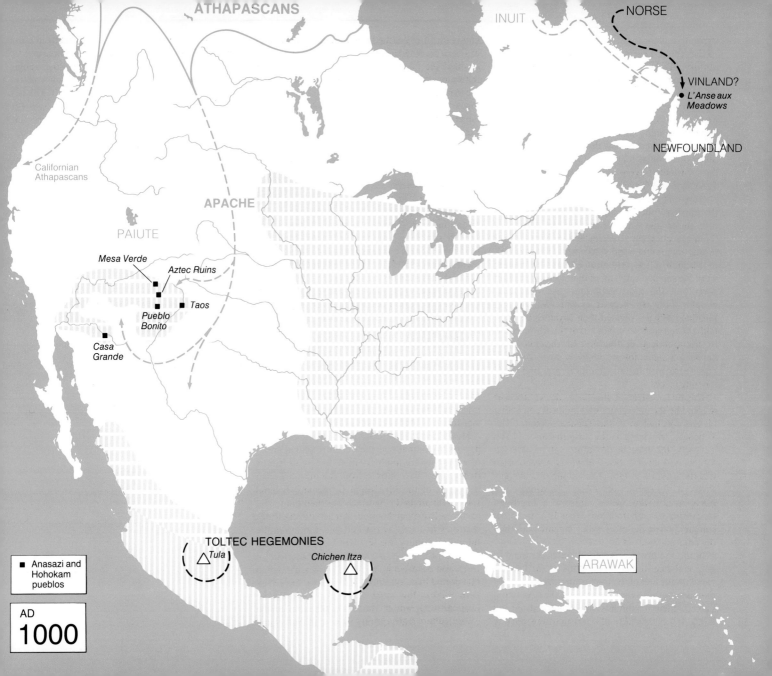

ATHAPASCANS

INUIT

NORSE

VINLAND?
*L'Anse aux
Meadows*

NEWFOUNDLAND

*Californian
Athapascans*

APACHE

PAIUTE

Mesa Verde

Aztec Ruins

■ *Taos*

*Pueblo
Bonito*

■ *Casa
Grande*

TOLTEC HEGEMONIES

△ *Tula*

Chichen Itza
△

ARAWAK

■ Anasazi and
Hohokam
pueblos

AD
1000

The Toltec hegemony collapsed in the twelfth century. We know nothing of the strife that must have accompanied this event and if there is any information on battles lost and chieftains overthrown in the hieroglyphic inscriptions of the time, we have as yet failed to find it. All we can say is that by the beginning of the thirteenth century both Tula and Chichen Itza lay deserted and that a new set of ceremonial centers had emerged. A few of these wielded considerable political power. Tenayuca, for example, had the allegiance of perhaps half the fifty-odd villages and townships in the Mexico Valley, Cempoala held a similar position among the Totanac peoples and Mayapan, though a poor copy of Chichen in architectural terms, apparently wielded a comparable authority in Yucatan. However, most of the new centers were too small to serve more than local needs, and several of the most important meso-American peoples – the Huastecs, Tarascans, Mixtecs and Highland Maya – divided their loyalties between half a dozen such sites. Nor is that the whole extent of the political devolution. In the interstices between these major peoples were scores of minor ones, each with its own traditions and traditional meeting places.

The first quarter of the fifteenth century was marked by the emergence of a political unit with a bit more weight to it, the Tepanec Empire. The Tepanecs, who lived on the western shore of Lake Texcoco, the lake in the center of the Mexico Valley, had several 'cities' of which Azcapotzalco was the most important. The empire was the personal achievement of Chief Tezozomoc of Azcapotzalco who, in the course of a long reign (according to oral tradition, from 1371 to 1426), conquered first the other valley communities then the adjacent areas of central Mexico.

In the south-western United States the trend to note is the continuing contraction of the farming zone. At the end of the thirteenth century many of the pueblos there were abandoned. They were not sacked, their inhabitants simply packed up and left. Just why they did and where they went nobody knows for sure, but the succession of droughts that has been recorded for the years 1276–99 must have strained the pueblo economy. Perhaps numbers fell so low that a new concentration was needed if the Apache were to be kept at bay. A bit later, towards the end of the fourteenth century, many of the Hohokam irrigation systems on the Gila River were similarly abandoned. Here again no one can be sure what happened. Perhaps the Hohokams moved west to the lower Colorado; perhaps they simply gave up the struggle to farm in the face of Apache harassment.

The set-back to farming in the south-west was local; in the rest of North America agriculture was on the increase. This was particularly true along the Mississippi where the full meso-American repertoire of maize, beans and squash was now in use. Hand in hand with this development go other signs of meso-American influence. The mounds built by the Mississippians had temples on top and, whatever beliefs had been involved in the 'Hopewell cult', the religion practised now was a meso-American style 'death cult'. The human sacrifices needed to sustain the ritual were doubtless obtained by cross-raiding. The raised anxieties that this created are apparent in the stockading with which contemporary communities surrounded themselves: for these early Americans the price of liberty was, in simple truth, eternal vigilance.

How does all this relate to the ethno-linguistic pattern? At some stage the north Iroquian group of tribes, which is a sub-group of the Greater Sioux family, must have moved from the macro-Siouan area west of the Mississippi to the area around Lakes Ontario and Erie which was their homeland in the early Colonial period. Archeology indicates that they had already reached this position in the thirteenth century, for, south of Lake Ontario, the remains of a group of long huts characteristic of Iroquoian culture have been radio-carbon dated to this period. The question is, how long have they been there? How much further back should we place their migration? The best bet seems to be the seventh- or eighth-century upheaval associated with the eastward spread of such overtly meso-American traits as full-scale farming, temple building and the death cult. However, it is also possible that the movement belongs to an even earlier period, the era of the Hopewell cult. It will be interesting to see if glottochronology (the study of rates of differentiation within language groups – in this instance Iroquoian) has anything to offer on this issue.

The map assumes that the southern Iroquoian peoples, of whom the Cherokee are the most important, moved in parallel with their relatives in the north. The assumption is not unreasonable but there is no evidence either way.

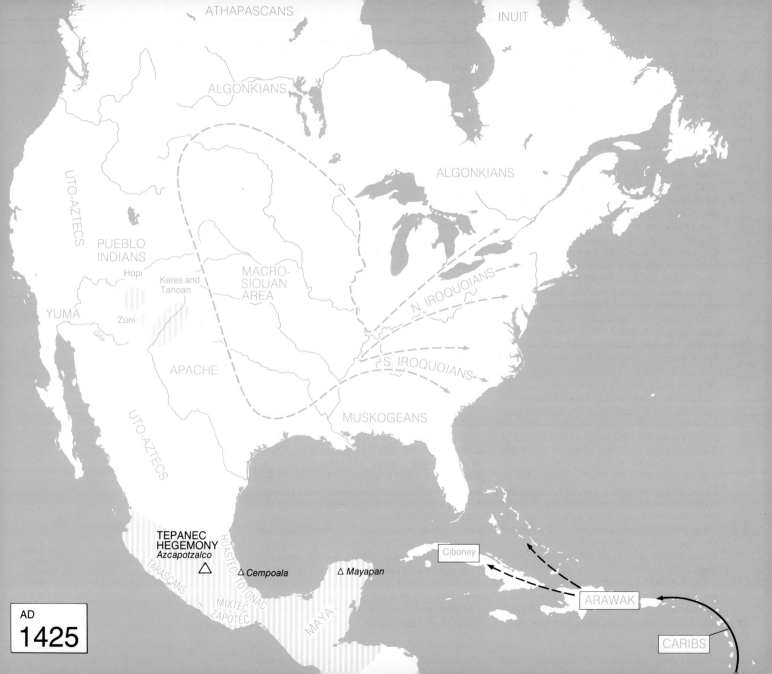

ATHAPASCANS

INUIT

ALGONKIANS

ALGONKIANS

UTO-AZTECS

PUEBLO
INDIANS

Hopi

Keres and
Tanoan

MACRO-
SIOUAN
AREA

N. IROQUOIANS

YUMA

Zuni

Gila

S. IROQUOIANS

APACHE

UTO-AZTECS

MUSKOGEANS

TARASCANS

TEPANEC
HEGEMONY
Azcapotzalco

HUASTEC TOTONAC

△

△ *Cempoala*

△ *Mayapan*

Ciboney

ARAWAK

MIXTEC
ZAPOTEC

MAYA

CARIBS

AD
1425

Christopher Columbus was born in Genoa, Italy, in 1451. As a young man he became involved in the great maritime adventure of the period, the exploration of the Atlantic coast of Africa. This was a Portuguese enterprise; its ultimate payoff was supposed to be the discovery of a route round Africa to the rich markets of the East. However, by the early 1480s it had become clear that Africa was so big that even if it was possible to sail round it, it would probably never be economic to do so.

What about the direct route to the East, across the Atlantic? The best geographical opinion of the time was that the distance was too great. Anything over 5,000 miles of open sea was more than contemporary ships could manage and the sort of figure involved in sailing from Europe to Japan or Indonesia was thought, quite correctly, to be more like 10,000 miles. But Columbus found an expert, Paolo Toscanelli of Florence, who was prepared to put forward a figure of 3,000 miles and this gave him the basic 'fact' he needed. After redoing the calculations himself and finding that, with a bit of nudging, the sum could be made to come out at 2,400 miles, he began trying to interest the crowned heads of Europe in his Transatlantic Plan. He put it to the King of Portugal (who said no in 1484, and again in 1488), the King of England (who said no in 1489), the King of France (who would not listen at all) and then to the two monarchs of Spain, Queen Isabella of Castile and her consort King Ferdinand of Aragon. Isabella said maybe, then no, and finally, in January 1492, yes.

By August of the same year Columbus had put his expedition together. It consisted of ninety men divided between three ships, the *Santa Maria* (100 tons), the *Pinta* (sixty tons) and the *Niña* (fifty tons). The flotilla set sail from the Canaries on 6 September. Three days later the last of the islands dropped below the horizon and the expedition was truly under way.

The crossing took thirty-three days. In the last week flocks of migrating birds flying west-south-west showed that land was near. Columbus, who had been sailing, or thought he had been sailing, due west till then, altered course to conform. Three days later, at 2 a.m. on the morning of 12 October, the lookout on the *Pinta* sighted land. It was one of the outermost islands of the Bahamas, most probably Samana Cay. By noon Columbus had found a safe anchorage, gone ashore and met his first Americans. Certain now that his theories were right and that he was somewhere in the Indonesian Archipelago, he called them Indians, and Indians they have remained ever since.[1]

The Indians, who probably had not been in the area for long themselves, indicated to Columbus that there were more and bigger islands to the south. Following their directions, he threaded his way through the Bahamas to Cuba, then sailed eastward along Cuba's northern coast to reach Hispaniola. This was the best populated of the Antilles and Columbus gathered in a presentable amount of gold in return for his trade goods. He also lost the *Santa Maria*, which grounded on a coral reef and had to be abandoned. Leaving twenty-one men behind to garrison a fort built out of the *Santa Maria*'s timbers, Columbus completed his journey along the north coast of Hispaniola and then, on 18 January 1493, headed for home. He was to have a terrible voyage through one of the worst storms of the decade and a justly rapturous reception from Isabella, her consort and her court.

The world that Columbus had opened up to European exploitation contained some 12 to 15 million 'Indians'. About half of them lived to the south of the area shown on the map and about 100,000, mostly Eskimo, to the north of it, in Alaska and the northern parts of Canada. Of the ones who did live in our area, most lived in Mexico, the majority of them in the central part of the country. If any Amerindians stood a chance against the Europeans it was these Mexicans. They had both the numbers and, particularly since the Aztecs had established their empire (for which see the next map), the capacity to mobilize them.

1 The natives that Columbus met called the island Guanahani: he renamed it San Salvador. A lot of ink has been spilled over the identity of San Salvador. The traditional favorite is Watling Island (which was officially renamed San Salvador in 1926) but recently computer simulations based on what survives of Columbus' log have shown that the island that best fits the available data is Samana Cay.

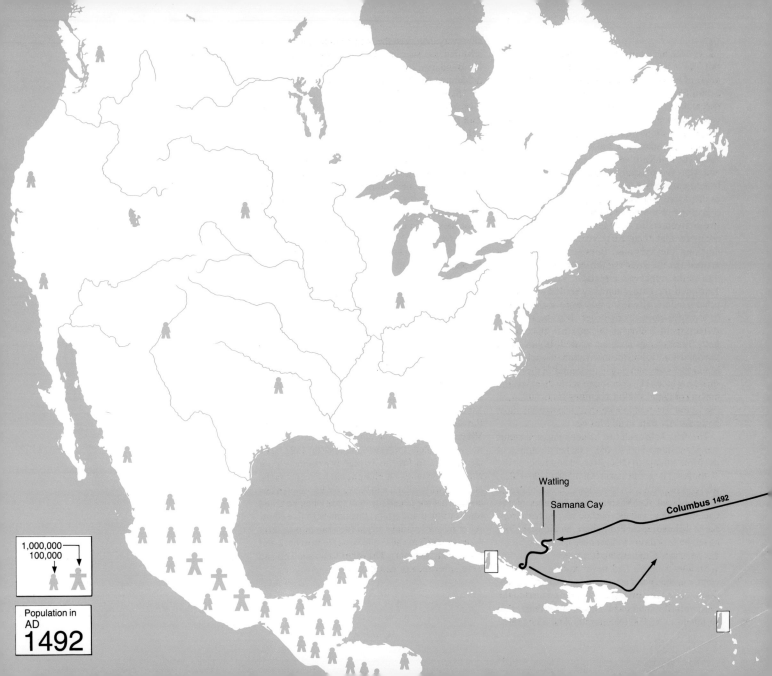

Watling

Samana Cay

Columbus 1492

1,000,000
100,000

Population in
AD
1492

Tepanec hegemony over the Mexico Valley did not long outlast Tezozomoc's reign. Within a few years of his death three local tributaries – Tenochtitlan, Texcoco and Tacuba – had combined forces, defeated the Tepanecs in battle and stormed their capital. Having laid Azcapotzalco waste, the three set up a new empire of their own. In theory this was run as a joint enterprise, but right from the start the Aztecs of Tenochtitlan dominated the partnership, and what was officially a 'triple alliance' was seen by contemporaries, and is remembered in history, as the Aztec Empire.

By their own account the Aztecs were comparative newcomers to the Mexico Valley. And they admitted that their early years there had been anything but glorious. Between the time they arrived (in the later twelfth century, apparently during the upheavals associated with the fall of Tula) and the date when they settled at Tenochtitlan (traditionally 1345) they were at the bottom of the Mexican pecking-order. But the time the Aztecs spent hiding in the marshes that ringed Lake Texcoco was not time wasted. It gave them the opportunity, and the motivation, to explore the island that was emerging in the center of the slowly shrinking lake. The decision to settle there was the making of them. Within a century Tenochtitlan, as the island site was known, had become the most powerful city state in all Mexico.

The first Aztec ruler to achieve imperial status was Moctezuma I (1440–68), who led the armies of the triple alliance to the Gulf coast and subdued the Totonacs. The greatest was Ahuitzotl (1486–1502), who conquered a corresponding area on the Pacific side, reduced the Mixtecs and Zapotecs of the Oaxaca Valley, and established his southern frontier at Tehuantepec. From there, in the year 1500, he led an expedition to Soconusco, on the present-day Mexican–Guatemalan frontier.

Middle America had never known as vast an empire as this, nor a metropolis as great as Tenochtitlan. Over the causeways that now connected the city with the mainland came the tribute that sustained its 80,000 inhabitants. And along these causeways marched the mournful files of prisoners destined for sacrifice, sometimes as many as a thousand in a single day.

Meanwhile, the Europeans were getting closer. In November 1493 Columbus returned to Hispaniola with seventeen ships and 1,200 men. The natives, outraged by constant demands for gold, had slaughtered the men he had left behind earlier in the year, but the colony Columbus now founded – at Isabela – was too strong to be eliminated in the same way. Indeed it was the Spanish who, over the next couple of years, established their control over the island. Columbus spent the first part of this period exploring Cuba and Jamaica. He did not get quite to the end of Cuba, which he decided was a promontory jutting out from the Asian mainland, and when he got back to Isabela the responsibilities of governorship prevented him from going exploring again. But he did make one further important discovery all the same. In 1498, on his way back from his next visit to Spain, he touched South America. Moreover, he realized from the size of the rivers he saw there that this previously uncharted land mass was of continental size.

The other significant voyage of this period was carried out by a countryman of Columbus, Giovanni Caboto, though, as he was working for the King of England, his name has come down to us in the Anglicized form of John Cabot. King Henry VII gave him a ship, the *Matthew* of Bristol, and in it Cabot sailed to Newfoundland in 1497. The documentation for this voyage is extremely poor and we know almost nothing about it except that he got to Newfoundland and back. We know even less about what happened the next year when he sailed for Newfoundland again, this time with five ships. After only a few days at sea they ran into a storm severe enough to cause one vessel to turn back and put into an Irish port. The other four sailed on and were never seen or heard of again.

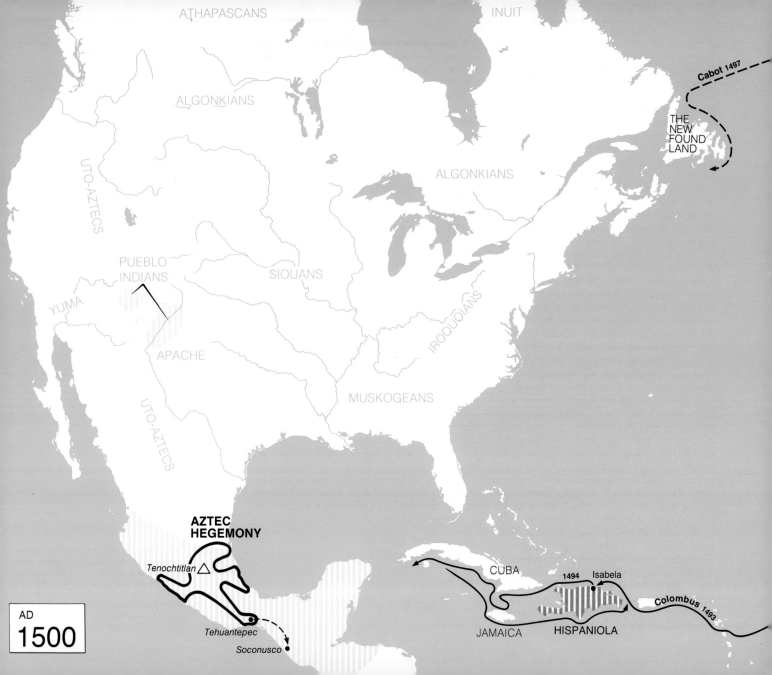

ATHAPASCANS

INUIT

Cabot 1497

THE
NEW
FOUND
LAND

ALGONKIANS

ALGONKIANS

UTO-AZTECS

PUEBLO
INDIANS

SIOUANS

YUMA

IROQUOIANS

APACHE

UTO-AZTECS

MUSKOGEANS

AZTEC
HEGEMONY

Tenochtitlan

CUBA

1494   Isabela

Colombus 1493

Tehuantepec

JAMAICA

HISPANIOLA

Soconusco

AD
1500

Columbus was not a success as Governor of Hispaniola. Some of this was not his fault, for Spaniards never like serving under a foreigner and did their best to make a difficult job impossible. But some of it was. A royal commissioner sent out to investigate the complaints lodged against him found enough of them true to justify drastic action. He stripped Columbus of his office, put him in irons and sent him back home for trial (October 1500).

Things did not end quite as badly as this. The charges against Columbus were not pressed and the Spanish sovereigns, though they would not reinstate him as governor, never lost faith in him as an explorer. In 1502, bearing their commission, he set off on his fourth and last voyage. This took him to Central America, initially to a point halfway along the coast of Honduras, then southward past Nicaragua and Costa Rica to Panama. By the time he turned for home it was clear to almost all on board that no one was going to get to China this way.

Unfortunately, it was not at all clear to Columbus. As far as he was concerned he had been sailing along the Malay Peninsula, and China had never been closer. But nobody was listening now. The explorer who had Europe's ear was Amerigo Vespucci and the tales he was telling were not of China but of South America. Vespucci was widely believed to have discovered this land and though this was not true – he cannot have been there before 1499, the year after Columbus – what he had done was realize its significance. Columbus tended to dismiss South America because it was irrelevant to his thesis. Vespucci stressed that this new land was far and away the most important of the discoveries so far. It was immense. It was also full of strange and wonderful things – exotic plants, peculiar animals and naked savages who practised cannibalism. It was, in a phrase, a New World. This was so self-evidently a correct assessment that when the German geographer Martin Waldseemüller proposed that, in honor of Amerigo, the new continent be named America, his suggestion was quickly adopted.

Waldseemüller's book and his map of 'America' were published in 1507. The true discoverer of the New World had died the year before, so we do not have his comments on either. It is a fair guess that he would have been just as incensed by the map, which showed a vast ocean between the New World and the eastern edge of Asia, as by Vespucci's false claim to priority. Columbus' achievement was that he changed everybody's world but his own.

The missing ocean, whose existence Waldseemüller had correctly deduced, was found by Balboa, who crossed over the Isthmus of Panama (off the bottom of our map) in 1513 and became the first European who ever 'star'd at the Pacific'. The same year saw important advances within the area of our map. Ponce de Leon, who had made his name conquering Puerto Rico, decided to investigate rumours of a large island to the north of Cuba which contained a 'fountain of youth' whose waters could restore old men to vigor. He set out from Puerto Rico, found and named Florida, and then, as nobody there had heard of the fountain, switched his search to the area west of Cuba. This leg of his voyage took him to Yucatan. Although there was no sign of the fountain there either, Ponce had acquired a sort of immortality. He had discovered both the United States and Mexico.

Not that he knew what he had done. He considered both Florida and Yucatan to be islands and, like most people at this stage, thought it more than possible that a way to China lay between them.[1]

Bermuda, which lies on the route favored by ships sailing from the West Indies to Spain, is named after one Juan Bermudez who happened on it on his way back from Hispaniola in 1505.

1 Ponce's earlier venture in Puerto Rico (1506) was one of three that the Spanish mounted to complete their control over the Greater Antilles, the others being Francisco de Garay's invasion of Jamaica (1509) and Diego Velasquez' invasion of Cuba (1511). On none of these islands did the natives, who were less numerous than those of Hispaniola, manage much in the way of resistance.

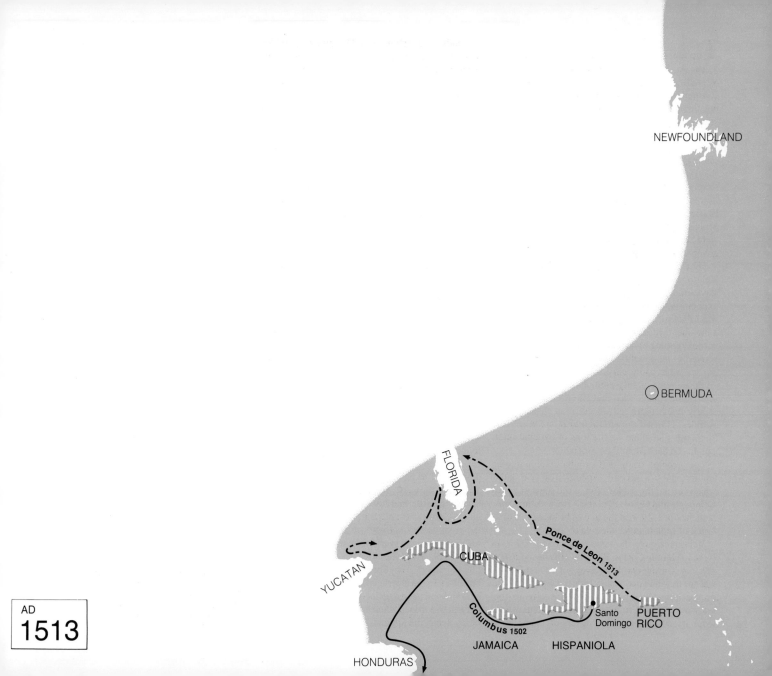

NEWFOUNDLAND

BERMUDA

FLORIDA

Ponce de Leon 1513

CUBA

YUCATAN

Columbus 1502

Santo
Domingo

PUERTO
RICO

JAMAICA

HISPANIOLA

HONDURAS

AD
1513

The native population of the Greater Antilles began to dwindle away as soon as the Spanish arrived. The Indians had little resistance to European diseases and the Spanish habit of rounding them up for forced labor compounded their vulnerability. Herded together, ill-treated and underfed, their numbers plummeted. The Spaniards tried to make good the deficiency by raiding the islands they had not occupied (notably the Bahamas and the Lesser Antilles) but this simply spread the circle of desolation wider. It was not until they hit on the idea of buying slaves from Black Africa that they began to get their labor problem under control. The first African slaves were landed at Hispaniola in 1505: by 1517 the governor was asking for a thousand a year.

That same year the Governor of Cuba, Diego Velasquez, decided to mount one of the old style slave raids against a new target, Yucatan. The expedition, headed by his lieutenant, Cordoba, was full of surprises. If Yucatan was an island it was a big one, for Cordoba sailed as far as Champoton without getting to the end of it. And its inhabitants proved to be doughty fighters: Cordoba's landing parties were badly cut up, losing the unprecedented number of fifty men. However, the really interesting thing was that these Indians were clearly much more 'advanced' than those of the Antilles. Hurried though their visit had been, the Spaniards had glimpsed the tops of pyramids and caught the flash of gold ornaments.

The general truth of Cordoba's account was confirmed by a second expedition a year later which carried the exploration of the coast as far as Cempoala and heard tell of the Aztecs. A third was launched in 1519 with the aim of bringing this new breed of Indian under the rule of Spain.

Velasquez gave the command of this 500-man force to Hernan Cortes. Precisely why he did so is a mystery, for the two had never got on and Cortes was to show him no loyalty. Indeed Cortes' first act on reaching Mexico was to found a 'city' (to be known as Vera Cruz) and accept a commission from its citizens (all two dozen of them) as a devious, if legal, way of repudiating Velasquez' authority. Having raised his own standard, Cortes then set about persuading the Totonacs of Cempoala to join him in a campaign against the Aztecs.

This took some doing as the Totonacs were terrified of the Aztecs. The Emperor Moctezuma II had not extended the Aztec Empire but he had consolidated it, campaigning regularly with all the ferocity for which Aztec armies were famous. Some tribes still held out against him, most notably the Tarascans and the Tlaxcalans, but those who had submitted were thoroughly cowed. In the case of the Cempoalans, Cortes neatly forced the issue by contriving the arrest and assisting in the escape of an Aztec embassy. Then, with the Cempoalans committed to his cause, he began his march inland.

Moctezuma, who seems to have thought this exotic newcomer could well be the hero Quetzalcoatl returning from his sojourn in the east, did not directly oppose his march, and the fiercest encounters the Spaniards had were with the Tlaxcalans. In the end they too accepted Cortes' offer of alliance and the tiny Spanish army, no more than 400 strong, approached the Aztec capital accompanied by some 6,000 Cempoalan and Tlaxcalan auxiliaries. Moctezuma let them all in, housing the Spaniards in one of the royal palaces.

As Cortes immediately perceived, the simplest way of obtaining control of Moctezuma's empire was to seize Moctezuma himself. This he soon found an excuse to do. His position was further strengthened when an expedition Velasquez had despatched to chastise his disobedient lieutenant arrived on the coast. Its leader proved no match for Cortes in battle and his men were soon marching under Cortes' banner. But, back in Tenochtitlan, the great *conquistador*'s luck was running out. In forbidding human sacrifice he not only earned the undying hatred of the priestly caste, but alienated the populace. The Spaniards found themselves boxed in by an outraged mob, and Moctezuma, who had managed to calm down trouble of this sort before, was stoned when he tried to do so again. As he lay dying, the Spaniards realized that, with little food, less water and no hope of getting further supplies of either, they had to pull out.

Retreat was not going to be easy. There were breaks in the causeways that connected the island of Tenochtitlan to the shore, and the bridges that normally spanned them had all been removed. But, once his mind was made up, Cortes wasted no time. He had a portable bridge constructed, detailed forty Tlaxcalans to carry it and, on the third night after Moctezuma's death, moved out quietly on to the western causeway. He actually got his entire force across the first gap unnoticed but at the second press the alarm was raised and in the subsequent press the portable bridge collapsed. The retreat turned into a shambles, remembered by veterans of the campaign as the *Noche Triste* (the 'Sad Night'). Half the Spaniards were cut down or captured, even heavier losses were sustained by their Indian allies. It was a beaten army that Cortes led out of the Mexico Valley which he had entered with such ambitious plans eight months before.

Cortes was not the only Spanish captain operating in Mexico, nor the only one in trouble: Piñeda, a henchman of Garay, the Governor of Jamaica, had landed among the Huastecs of the north-east in 1520. They quickly overwhelmed his small force and he and many of his men were made prisoner. So much for Garay's idea that the Gulf offered easy pickings, and so much for his lieutenant too, for that matter. But if Piñeda's end atop a Huastec pyramid was ignominious, he has his place in history. Before landing, he had sailed the Gulf coast from Florida to Mexico, proving that both formed part of the same land mass. Clearly there was a North American continent as well as a South American one.

ATHAPASCANS

INUIT

ALGONKIANS

ALGONKIANS

UTO-AZTECS

PUEBLO
INDIANS

SIOUANS

YUMA

APACHE

IROQUOIANS

UTO-AZTECS

MUSKOGEANS

Piñeda
1519–20

AZTEC
HEGEMONY

Tlaxcala

Cortes
1519

Havana

SPANISH ANTILLES

Tenochtitlan

Vera Cruz

Cempoala

Champoton

CUBA

HISPANIOLA

PUERTO
RICO

JAMAICA

AD
1520

Cortes' Tlaxcalan allies stood by him in his hour of need. They gave him and his men food and shelter, and he repaid them by settling such scores as they had with their neighbors. The Spaniards recovered their morale in these local campaigns, while their numbers were restored when two ships despatched by the Governor of Jamaica for the succour of Piñeda put in at Vera Cruz. With Piñeda dead and his enterprise in ruins, the newcomers decided to throw in their lot with Cortes. They formed a major part of his army when, in April 1521, he marched for a second time against Tenochtitlan.

This time Cortes moved slowly and methodically. First he built a flotilla of small ships which gave him command of the lake. Then he advanced assault teams along all three of the causeways simultaneously. For three months the Spaniards fought their way across the city, moving forward house by house, pulling down each building as they cleared it. At the end of this period Cortes was master of Tenochtitlan (temporarily ruined, but soon to be rebuilt as Mexico City) and of the Aztec Empire (which his lieutenants were able to occupy without significant opposition). Essentially the conquest of Mexico – New Spain, as the Spanish called it – was complete.

Central America was next. Cortes had to move fast here because the Spaniards in Panama were now advancing north – they had already invaded Costa Rica. In 1523 Cortes sent his lieutenant Alvarado down the Pacific Coast to Guatemala and the next year he himself set out for Honduras. He had already despatched a small force there by sea, but this had been suborned by his old enemy, Governor Velasquez of Cuba. With contingents from Panama and Hispaniola hovering around as well, it looked as if Honduras was going to become a cockpit for all the rival conquistador groups.

Cortes was more interested in the lands south of Mexico than in those to the north because that is where the people were, and people had turned out to be Middle America's only significant asset. The sack of Tenochtitlan had yielded very little in the way of treasure – not even enough to buy fresh horses for the cavalry – and if Cortes were to pay off his followers as he had promised, it could only be with Indian serfs. Land without Indians to work it was worth nothing to a Spaniard, whereas an estate with built-in labor conferred not only wealth (in kind if not in cash) but something that was equally important, status.

Back in Europe it was the area north of Mexico that was attracting the interest. Magellan and del Cano's famous circumnavigation had shown that there was a western route to the Indies (the real ones, the East Indies). But what it had also shown was that this particular route – via the straits Magellan had discovered at the tip of South America – was not a very useful one. It could never be competitive with Portugal's eastward passage. What was needed was a strait somewhere in the unexplored stretch between Newfoundland and Florida. Both the French and the Spanish decided to send ships to search these latitudes.

The French were quicker off the mark. The Italian navigator they employed, Giovanni de Verrazano, set sail in early 1524 and was back with the bad news by midsummer. From his landfall at Cape Fear he had followed the coast north to Newfoundland without finding anything in the way of a passage. He had not sailed all that close in. He had entered New York Bay (and anchored where the bridge named after him now stands) and Narragansett Bay (where he remarked that nearby Block Island looked rather like the Mediterranean island of Rhodes) but he had completely missed the entrances to Chesapeake Bay, Delaware Bay and the Bay of Fundy. Nevertheless, he seems to have had no doubt that the coastline he was sailing was a continuous one.[1]

1 Verrazano compromised on this when he got home. His report to the French king makes considerable play of the fact that when he was sailing along the Carolina Banks he could see nothing but water on the far side. Could not this 'Sea of Verrazano' be an arm of the Pacific? Anyone as familiar with the Venetian Lagoon as Verrazano surely was, must have known the right answer to this question, and the fact that he did not waste any time searching the banks for openings (and there are plenty of them) shows that he knew perfectly well what sand bars like these signified. Presumably his second thoughts were inspired by hopes of obtaining a new commission but, if so, they failed in their object. No one in authority took his 'sea' seriously (though some cartographers did) and no follow-up expeditions were sent to the banks.

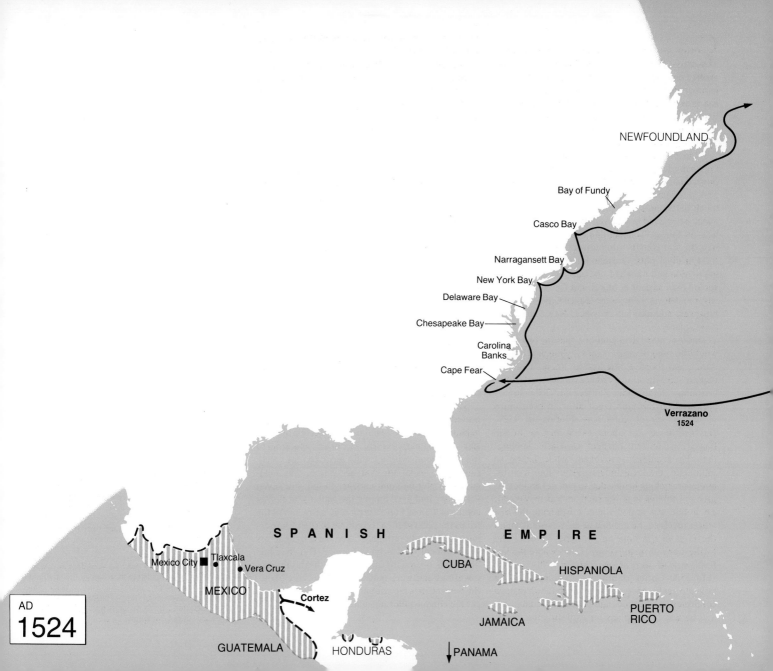

NEWFOUNDLAND

Bay of Fundy

Casco Bay

Narragansett Bay

New York Bay

Delaware Bay

Chesapeake Bay

Carolina
Banks

Cape Fear

Verrazano
1524

S P A N I S H   E M P I R E

CUBA

HISPANIOLA

Mexico City
Tlaxcala
Vera Cruz

Cortez

MEXICO

JAMAICA

PUERTO
RICO

AD
1524

GUATEMALA

HONDURAS

↓ PANAMA

Cortes should never have gone to Honduras. The march there was hard and long and when he arrived he found that his supporters had the upper hand anyway. Meanwhile he had lost out in Mexico. Jealous Spaniards had petitioned the Crown to revoke his governorship, and the Crown had agreed to suspend it, forcing Cortes to return to Spain to argue his case (1528).

While he was away one of his enemies, Nuno de Guzman, decided that he too could play the *conquistador*. An Indian had told him that off to the east, or maybe north-east, were tribes that offered much better prospects for plunder than the Mexicans. They lived in seven cities, each one of which was as big as Tenochtitlan, and they were so wealthy that even the common people cooked their food in silver pots. Guzman put together a major expedition and marched first east, then north. He spilled a great deal of blood, but found very little silver and never a one of the 'Seven Cities'. He did, however, add another province, New Galicia, to New Spain.

This was more than could be said for two other would-be *conquistadors*. Louis Ayllon died in 1526 during an abortive attempt to found a colony named San Miguel somewhere on the coast of the Carolinas. And Panfilo Narvaez and 300 men disappeared on the Gulf coast after an even more disastrous try at colonizing Florida in 1527. Narvaez made just about every mistake in the book. First he sent his fleet away after landing, then he needlessly provoked, while failing to intimidate, the local Indians. After four months' aimless marching he decided to pull out and set his men to cobbling together such craft as they could. Their fate was sealed when, misjudging the distances involved, he decided to sail westward round the Gulf in the hope of reaching Mexico. The furthest any of them got was Texas where the last few boatloads were shipwrecked in 1528.

In 1530 Cortes returned to Mexico. He had failed to get his governorship back but he had been confirmed in his estates and his military command, and he was full of plans for exploring the Pacific coast. He personally led the expedition that discovered (lower) California in 1533 and he would have done more if the Viceroy of New Spain, Antonio de Mendoza, had not forbidden it. The office of viceroy, created in 1535, conferred authority over every corner of Spain's American Empire.[1]

The viceroy claimed authority even further afield than this. Regardless of whether they were in effective occupation or not, the Spaniards considered that the entire New World (except Brazil, on which there was a special agreement with the Portuguese) belonged to them by right of discovery. According to them, the viceroy's writ ran from Labrador to Tierra del Fuego. Challenging this view were the French and English who recognized Spain's title only where Spanish rule was established. And the French were now beginning to take an interest in North America. In 1534 the French king commissioned Jacques Cartier of St Malo to search for a passage to China, and Cartier chose to look for it on the far side of Newfoundland. That year he charted most of the Gulf of St Lawrence: the next he sailed up the river to the Huron villages of Stadacona (modern Quebec) and Hochelaga (Montreal). He wintered at Hochelaga and returned home determined to plant a colony there one day.

Spanish interest in the area north of Mexico, muted since the disappointments of Guzman's expedition, now received an unexpected fillip. A slave-raiding party returned from an expedition to the Rio Sonora with a totally unlooked-for catch, four survivors of the Narvaez fiasco. The emaciated quartet had quite a story to tell. For seven years they had lived among the Indians, at first as captives, then as wandering medicine-men. All the tribes they had seen in the course of their journeyings, which had eventually taken them right across the continent, had been very poor. But they had heard talk of Indians off to the north who lived in townships and were much richer. So, very likely, the Seven Cities did exist after all. It was enough to get the conquistador itch going again.[2]

1 The distinction here is between the Viceroyalty of New Spain and the province of the same name which was merely one of five (New Spain, New Galicia, Yucatan, Guatemala and the Islands) under the viceregal authority.

Spanish control over Yucatan and Guatemala was much less complete than the map makes it look. Yucatan was not even nominally pacified until 1543 and both in Yucatan and Guatemala vast areas of the interior remained outside the purviews of the administration for the entire colonial period.

The government of the islands operated from Santo Domingo. It moved there from Isabela, which had proved unhealthy, in 1496.

2. The four survivors were Cabeza de Vaca, who, as senior officer, gets his name attached to this involuntary expedition, two other Spaniards and a black named Esteban, of whom more later. The exact route the four took is uncertain, the more so as no one knows for sure where they started out from.

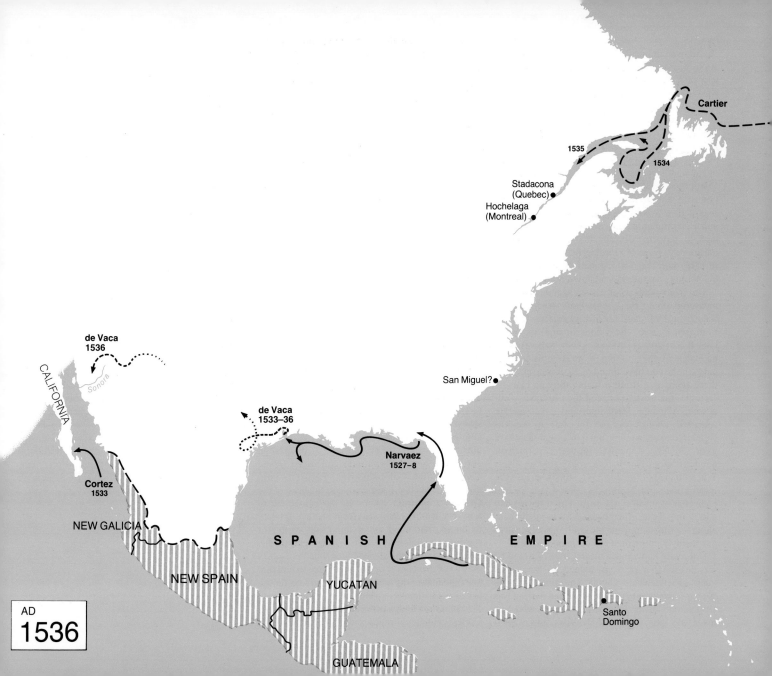

Cartier

1535

1534

Stadacona
(Quebec) ●

Hochelaga
(Montreal) ●

de Vaca
1536

CALIFORNIA

Sonora

San Miguel? ●

de Vaca
1533–36

Narvaez
1527–8

Cortez
1533

NEW GALICIA

S P A N I S H   E M P I R E

NEW SPAIN

YUCATAN

Santo
Domingo

GUATEMALA

AD
1536

The two tall tales that had lured the first generation of *conquistadors* – the one about the Fountain of Youth that had led Ponce de Leon and Narvaez to Florida, and the one about the 'Seven Cities' rich in silver sought unsuccessfully by Nuno de Guzman – were given their final airing in the 1540s. De Vaca's report indicated that the Seven Cities were perhaps to be found due north of Mexico in the unexplored lands that now form part of the south-western United States. In February 1540 Francisco de Coronado set out in this direction with what by New World standards could be regarded as a considerable army: 400 Spaniards and 1,300 Indian auxiliaries. Meanwhile, Hernan de Soto, governor of Cuba, had mounted a reconnaissance in force of Florida which was eventually to carry him and his 570-man expedition across much of the south-eastern United States.

The commanders of these expeditions fully measured up to the *conquistador* tradition. De Soto, who had made his fortune at the elbow of Francisco Pizarro, the conqueror of Peru, was a born leader and as ruthless as they come: if there had been anything to find in the American southlands, he would have found it. As it was, he spent three years on a fruitless march through Florida, Georgia, the western edge of the Carolinas, Tennessee, Alabama, Mississippi and Arkansas. He squeezed enough out of the Indians he encountered to keep going, but it was clear that there were too few of them to support a permanent administration. Nor had they any gold or silver. When he died of fever in 1542, somewhere on the lower Mississippi, he must have known that he had been chasing a will-o'-the-wisp. The survivors had a look into Texas, then headed for home by boat along the Mississippi and the Gulf coast of Mexico. Surprisingly, more than 300 of them made it.

Coronado had a much clearer idea of where he was headed than de Soto. Indeed, he thought he knew exactly where Cibola, the nearest of the 'Seven Cities' was to be found. He had sent out two scouts, one being Esteban, the black who had made the long walk with de Vaca, the other a Franciscan missionary named Brother Marcos. Esteban did remarkably well. His medicine-man act so awed the Indians he met that they rapidly passed him on to the nearest 'city' they knew of, the Zuni pueblo of Hawikuh. Unfortunately, the Zuni were not so easily impressed. They took one look at this black man talking about white Gods, decided he was either mad or bad and killed him. Brother Marcos brought the news back to Mexico. By his account he had followed Esteban to Cibola (meaning Hawikuh: where he got the name from no one knows) and though he had not actually entered the city he had seen enough to speak with confidence of its many splendors. Coronado's men set out in high spirits.

Their good humor did not last long once they arrived at Hawikuh. Had they marched a thousand miles to sack a miserable little pueblo whose wretched inhabitants had scarcely a golden nose-plug between them? By the blood of Our Lady they had not. A few words with Brother Marcos seemed in order, but even in this the hapless soldiery were to be frustrated. Seeing how things were going, the talkative little friar had high-tailed it back to Mexico.

Coronado refused to be discouraged. He led the main force eastward to the cluster of pueblos on the upper Rio Grande, then on a long foray across the Great Plains where, for the first time, Europeans set eyes on the tepees of the buffalo-hunting tribes. One of his lieutenants exploring in the opposite direction passed by the Hopi country to discover an even more amazing sight, the mile-deep Grand Canyon of the Colorado river. Earlier a third expedition had been despatched to the head of the Gulf of California where it was supposed to rendezvous with a fleet sent from Mexico. It failed to do so, but filled in an important corner of American geography. Alas, geographical discoveries and natural wonders line no one's pockets. Coronado returned to Mexico to find that his expedition was accounted a complete failure because it had not recovered any of its costs.

Exploration by sea proved equally unrewarding. Cortes' lieutenant Francisco de Ulloa charted both faces of peninsular California in 1539–40. Two years later one of the viceroy's men, Juan Rodriguez Cabrillo, took two ships up the coast of California proper as far as Bodega Bay. Cabrillo had no way of knowing that behind one of the banks of cloud hugging the shoreline lay the entrance to the splendid harbor of San Francisco Bay, and on winter's approach he pulled back to San Miguel Island (opposite present-day Santa Barbara) where he succumbed to a wound received earlier. In the spring his successor in command, Bartolomeo Ferrer, led the expedition north again, ultimately reaching a point not far short of the present California–Oregon border. From there he managed to make it back to Mexico, but only after taking such a fearful battering from mountainous seas that no one was inclined to repeat the exercise.

One more tale of failure remains to be told, the French attempt to establish a colony in Canada in 1541. Jacques Cartier, returning to the St Lawrence for the third time, chose a site a short distance upstream from Stadacona (Quebec). He named it Charlesbourg-Royal and he and his 150 followers successfully defended it against the Huron through that winter. But by spring 1542 morale was ebbing fast, there was no sign of promised reinforcements and Cartier decided to take the survivors (half the original number?) back to France. Off Newfoundland he met the much delayed follow-up expedition but even this did not make him change his mind. He sailed off, leaving the reinforcements to reoccupy the Charlesbourg-Royal site on their own, suffer the same privations and come to the same conclusion. By September 1543 they too were back in France.

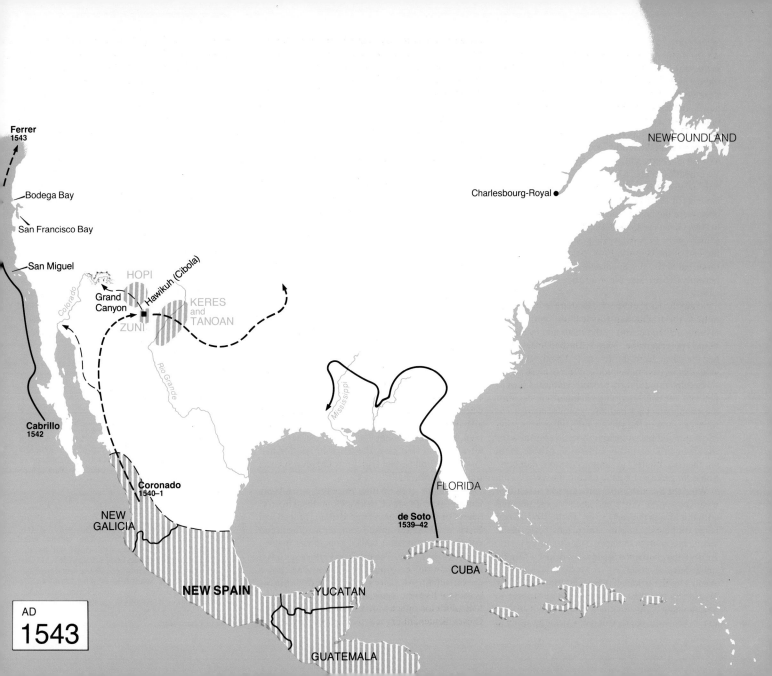

Ferrer
1543

Bodega Bay

San Francisco Bay

San Miguel

NEWFOUNDLAND

Charlesbourg-Royal ●

HOPI

Colorado

Grand
Canyon

Hawikuh (Cibola)

KERES
and
TANOAN

ZUNI

Rio Grande

Cabrillo
1542

Mississippi

Coronado
1540–1

FLORIDA

de Soto
1539–42

NEW
GALICIA

CUBA

NEW SPAIN

YUCATAN

GUATEMALA

AD
1543

If the 1540s were disappointing to the Spaniards in one way – it was pretty clear from the accounts of the de Soto and Coronado expeditions that there were no more native empires to be discovered, no more sources of easy plunder – they more than made up for it in another. During the course of the decade rich deposits of silver, far richer than any known in the Old World, were discovered in both Mexico and Peru. The richest strike of all was in the Viceroyalty of Peru, where a veritable silver mountain was discovered at Potosi (in present-day Bolivia) in 1545. Less bountiful, but still considerable, were the finds made in and around Zacatecas in New Galicia in 1546–8. Between them these two sources were to boost world production sixfold by the end of the century. From being poor in everything but serfs, the Spaniards of the New World became rich in just the way they wanted, hard cash.[1]

So did the King of Spain. His share in the mines' output, the traditional 'Royal Fifth', boosted his revenues by 10 percent in the 1560s and by no less than 33 percent in the 1590s. All he had to do was to get the silver from the Indies to Spain. This was actually less easy than it looked. French privateers – warships fitted out by private syndicates – were picking off an alarming number of Spanish merchantmen. They had, for example, managed to hijack several of the vessels charged with carrying the Aztec and Inca treasures to Spain. And news of the silver strikes was bound to bring privateers on to the sea routes in unprecedented numbers. Something had to be done to stop them.

What the Spanish authorities did was to institute a convoy system. They had already experimented with this idea in the early 1540s. In the 1560s, when silver shipments became important, they made sailing in convoy mandatory. Ships trading with the Indies – they had to be Spanish, of course – formed up in Seville, departing in May for Mexico and August for the Isthmus. After wintering in the New World the two fleets rendezvoused at Havana in March and returned to Spain via the Florida Channel, the North Atlantic and the Azores. The system worked well. Thirty or so merchantmen and half a dozen men-of-war, which was the size of the average home-bound convoy, was too large a force for the privateers to take on. Convoying might cause delays, and it was certainly costly, but it protected Spain's monopoly position in the New World and it got the king's silver safely home.[2]

The Spanish colonists were less happy with the system. They had to buy from government-licensed traders and they found themselves poorly served. Manufactures tended to be shoddy, overpriced and in short supply. Slaves were rarely available in the numbers needed. Spain's economy, never one of Europe's most efficient, was visibly floundering. An outdated class system, an overambitious foreign policy, an overstretched bureaucracy and the inflationary effects of the silver for which so much else was sacrificed, all contributed to the decline. Everything was behind schedule, and quite likely would never happen at all.

Given this situation, it is no wonder that when interlopers like John Hawkins, a merchant from Plymouth, England, showed up with a cargo of slaves, Spanish settlers bought the lot without worrying too much about licenses. Hawkins netted a handsome profit from his voyages of 1562–3 and 1564–6 and even on his third voyage, in 1568–70, when he had the misfortune to run foul of an arriving convoy and lost his flagship and most of his men, he still made money. Clearly if market forces were allowed free play, the English, and for that matter the French and Dutch, would give Spanish traders a hard time.

One major New World resource already lay outside Spain's control, the Newfoundland fishery. Scores of fishing smacks from Britain, France and Iberia spent the spring and summer hauling in cod on the Newfoundland banks, sometimes making two voyages a year. The catch was either salted on board, in which case the fishermen returned home direct, or taken on shore and cured by drying in the sun. The French, Spanish and Portuguese, who had plenty of salt, favored the first method. The British, whose climate was too gloomy for salt pans to be a practical proposition, opted for sun drying. As a result the British, though in a minority in the fishing fleet, were in a majority among the fishermen camping ashore.

Though the Newfoundland banks formed the focus of the fisheries active at this time, it is worth noting two smaller enterprises. One is the whaling industry developed by the Basques in the Strait of Belle Isle. For centuries the Basques had been hunting the right whales as they passed through the Bay of Biscay. The parallel migration along the American coast provided them with an opportunity which they were quick to exploit. Occasionally the ice caught these whalers at their shore stations, but it was never their intention to winter in Labrador and many of those who did were killed by the cold. Cod fishermen operating in the Gulf of St Lawrence form the second group. Most of them were French. The important thing about them is that they supplemented their earnings by trading with the local Indians. They gave them iron tools and in return the Indians – Montagnais, Micmac – gave them furs. It was the beginning of an important traffic.

1 The Viceroyalty of Peru, covering all South America bar Brazil, was set up in 1542. Its foundations had been laid in the previous decade when Francesco Pizarro, in a campaign that has many parallels with Cortes' conquest of Mexico, overthrew the native ruler of Peru, Inca Athualpa.

2 The French privateers were handicapped by the failure of their attempts to establish bases on the Atlantic coast of North America. The first, Charlesfort on Parris Island, South Carolina, was abandoned within a few months of its foundation (1562). The second, Fort Caroline in northern Florida, was wiped out by the Spanish the year after it had been set up (1564–5). The episode is remembered mainly because the threat from the French prompted the Spanish to establish forts of their own in the area, namely St Augustine, Florida, founded in 1565, which makes it the oldest continuously inhabited European settlement in North America, and St Elena, on the site of Charlesfort.

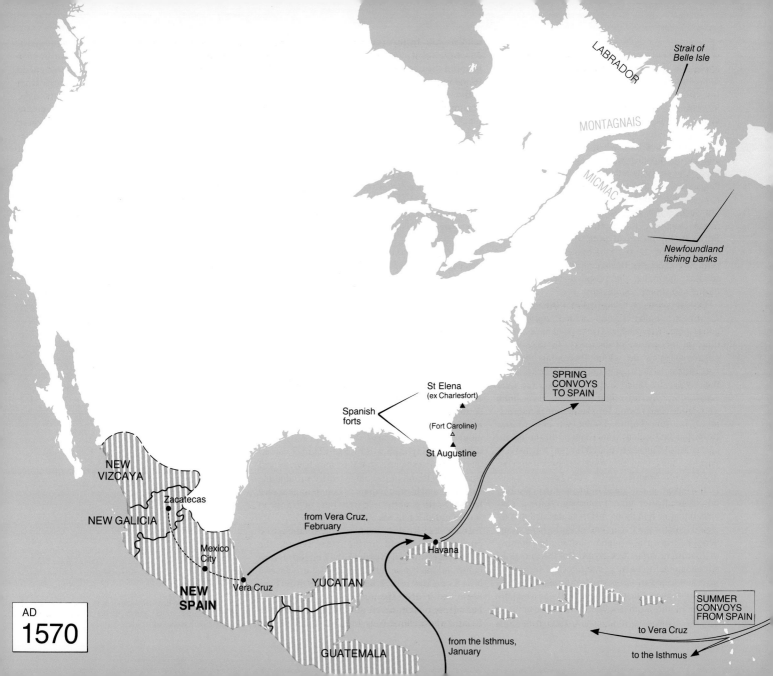

LABRADOR

Strait of Belle Isle

MONTAGNAIS

MICMAC

Newfoundland fishing banks

SPRING CONVOYS TO SPAIN

St Elena
(ex Charlesfort) ▲

Spanish forts

(Fort Caroline) △

St Augustine ▲

NEW VIZCAYA

Zacatecas ●

NEW GALICIA

Mexico City ●

NEW SPAIN

Vera Cruz ●

from Vera Cruz, February

YUCATAN

Havana ●

from the Isthmus, January

GUATEMALA

SUMMER CONVOYS FROM SPAIN

to Vera Cruz

to the Isthmus

AD **1570**

John Hawkins seems to have been philosophical about his defeat at Vera Cruz. He knew the Spaniards regarded all interlopers as enemies of the state and he accepted the verdict of the battle he was forced to fight. His cousin and fellow captain Francis Drake felt very differently. On the grounds that they had negotiated when they were weak and struck hard when they were strong, he charged the Spanish with treachery and called on God, Queen Elizabeth and his countrymen for vengeance. He also took some practical measures towards this end himself. In a series of raids that left such major Spanish colonial settlements as Santo Domingo, the capital of Hispaniola, and Porto Bello, the main port of the Isthmus, in smoking ruins, Drake hurt Spain, lined his own pockets and created the legend of the Elizabethan sea-dog, humbling the proud dons by superior daring and superb seamanship.

Though most of his activities focused on the Caribbean sea-lanes and added nothing to geographical knowledge, Drake does have a small place in the history of discovery. In 1577–80 he circumnavigated the globe, becoming the first Englishman to do so, and during the Pacific leg of this voyage he sailed further north on the west coast of America than anyone had done previously. The reason for the detour is interesting. The year before Drake set out, Martin Frobisher had sailed from England to the northeast coast of Canada to search for the 'North-West Passage', the fabled easy route to China round the top of North America. After a brief exploration of Baffin Island, in particular of the mouth of the Bay now named after him, Frobisher returned convinced that he had found it. Drake decided that he would look for the Pacific end of Frobisher's strait, hence his trip up the Oregon coast. Finding nothing of interest, he soon turned back. But the story does not end there for, twenty years later, a Greek pilot, who had sailed in the service of Spain under the name of Juan de Fuca, claimed to have reached the mouth of the strait for which Drake had been looking. That was in 1592 and, though modern scholars are highly sceptical about his entirely uncorroborated account, enough people have believed the tale for the strait south of Vancouver Island to bear his name today.

Between looking for a new route to Cathay and beating up the Spanish colonials, the English found time for a third American enterprise, the founding of a colony. The idea was Sir Walter Raleigh's. With Queen Elizabeth's blessing, Raleigh despatched an expedition to the stretch of the coastline between Florida and Norumbega (as New England was known at this time), a coast that he dubbed Virginia in honor of the unwed and ever-hesitant queen. The location chosen for the colony was Roanoke Island, in what is now North Carolina. In 1585, 108 colonists landed there with high hopes of attaining self-sufficiency and promises of regular supply till they did so. They were disappointed in both, and when Drake happened by the next year the survivors were in such a pitiful state that he agreed to take them home. In 1587 Raleigh tried again at the same spot, promising all concerned that this time the back-up would be good enough to sustain the colony through any early difficulties. But the next year was the year of the Armada, Spain's majestic response to a decade of English impertinences, and every ship the queen could lay her hands on was needed for the defense of the realm. Not till 1590 did a relief ship get through to Roanoke, only to find the village site deserted. Nobody knows what happened to the colonists, though the word CROATOAN carved on a door post suggests that they may have moved to a nearby island of this name before succumbing to disease and hostile Indians. Their disappearance left the North American coast as bare of European settlement as it had been a century earlier.

While the English failed in their attempt to establish a foothold in the New World, the Spaniards continued to enlarge their already formidable and mighty empire. In 1596 the province of New Leon was established to the north of New Spain and in 1598 the pueblos of the upper Rio Grande were conquered and organized into the isolated province of New Mexico. But even the Spanish could do nothing with the Atlantic coast. The outpost at St Elena was withdrawn in 1586 following a raid by Drake (the same one that ended with his rescue of the first set of colonists from Roanoke) and thereafter St Augustine marked the northern limit of Spanish power. In fact there were no other Europeans permanently ashore anywhere north of St Augustine until 1600, when a Frenchman engaged in the fur trade founded a post at Tadoussac on the St Lawrence.[1]

1 This refers to the mainland. There were a few French on Sable Island, ninety miles off Nova Scotia, servicing ships engaged in the fur trade.

Vancouver Island

Strait of
Juan de Fuca

Drake
1579

Tadoussac
(French)

Sable Island
(French)

NORUMBEGA

NEW
MEXICO

VIRGINIA

Roanoke Island

St Augustine
(Spanish)

FLORIDA

NEW
VIZCAYA

NEW
LEON

NEW
GALICIA

NEW SPAIN

YUCATAN

CUBA

JAMAICA   HISPANIOLA

Santo
Domingo

PUERTO
RICO

AD
1600

GUATEMALA

In 1607 the English made another attempt to plant a colony in Virginia. Three ships, the *Susan Constant, Godspeed* and *Discovery* landed 102 settlers on the James Peninsula at a site roughly 100 miles to the north of Raleigh's Roanoke venture of twenty years before. The operation was better planned and executed than Raleigh's, with supply and reinforcement vessels arriving regularly during the next few years. None the less, mortality among the colonists was so high that by the spring of 1610 they had all had enough. Of the 600 who had been put ashore, barely 200 were still alive and that included 100 who had just arrived. A vote to return home was carried unanimously.

The Jamestown colony was saved by the arrival of Lord de la Warr with a further 150 settlers. He ordered the colonists, who had already embarked for the homeward voyage, back to 'James City', placed the entire settlement under martial law and refused to discuss the possibility of failure. An iron hand was certainly needed. The mortality rate remained as high as ever, with less than half of new arrivals surviving their first twelve months in America, and many of those who did getting picked off by hostile Indians. Because there were relatively few women, the birth rate was negligible. Consequently to survive at all the colony needed constant reinforcement. But survive it did. By 1615 the Virginia Company had its toe-hold in the New World: it had even discovered, in the cultivation of tobacco, a means of getting some return on its investment.

The French were also active in North America at this time. They were making good money from the fur trade and, though they were far from convinced that a full-scale colony was either necessary or desirable, they decided to tighten their grip on the traffic by establishing strong points ashore. Their first enterprise of this type, an outpost at Isle Ste Croix on the Bay of Fundy, was abandoned the next year in favor of Port Royal on the opposite side of the bay (1605). After an equally shaky start, Port Royal attained a modest success, giving substance to the French claim to sovereignty over Acadia.

Much more significant than this Acadian venture was the founding of Quebec by Champlain in 1608. Quebec was well placed to act as an entrepôt for the traffic in furs, particularly as regards its richest component, the peltry collected by the Huron from the area north of the Great Lakes. When the Huron were able to get their canoes safely through to Quebec, the fortunes of the French were made.

The trouble was that the Huron did not always get through. There was a long-standing enmity between them and the Iroquois Confederacy, the 'Five Nations' of upstate New York. This was not based on anything tangible. The Huron belonged to the same Iroquoian ethno-linguistic group as the Five Nations and were, like them, relatively recent intruders into the region (see map AD 1425). In theory they were, like the Iroquois proper, more sophisticated and socially cohesive than the local Algonkians – the Algonkin to the north of Quebec and the Montagnais of the lower St Lawrence. In practice they proved so far inferior to the Five Nations in discipline and determination that they were unable to stand up to them on the battlefield. In allying themselves with the Huron against the Iroquois, the French had picked a loser.

Not that the French had any choice, for it was the Huron, not the Iroquois, who had the furs. And anyway, the initial battles with the Iroquois did not go too badly. The French had guns and the 1609 campaign, in the course of which Champlain discovered the lake now named after him, was a distinct success. But a major effort in 1615 was ruined by the indecision of the Huron and merely earned the French the undying hatred of the Mohawks, the most powerful of the Five Nations.

In the course of the 1615 campaign Champlain visited the nearer two of the Great Lakes, Huron and Ontario. He was not the first European to see them for that title had already been gained by a protégé of his, Etienne Brulé, who had visited Lake Huron as early as 1611. Now Brulé not only led the way to Lake Ontario but, by his own account, traveled from there to the Susquehanna and then down this river to Chesapeake Bay. The contrast in style between these individual French-

men probing the continent via its waterways, and the English colonists bunched up on the James Peninsula, could hardly be more striking.

Where the English excelled was in maritime exploration, and in Henry Hudson of Bristol they had a man of the same mettle as Champlain and Brulé. In 1607 Hudson was hired by a Dutch company that was looking at the practicality of the 'North-East Passage', a route to China along the northern rim of Asia. In 1609 he took it on himself to try the north-west alternative in an extempore voyage that took him to the North American coast at a mid-Atlantic level. He entered the Verrazzano narrows and explored the Hudson River as far north as present-day Albany before concluding, from the absence of tides, that this was not going to lead him to the Pacific. The next year, with the backing of an English syndicate, he tried again in the high latitudes where the North-West Passage was normally sought. He found the entrance to Hudson Bay and sailed down its eastern shore to James Bay. There, in early 1611, his crew mutinied and put him and eight others in an open boat. The mutineers made it safely back to England, but no trace has ever been found of Hudson and his companions.

Hudson's discoveries are the last important spin-offs of the search for the North-West Passage which was now drawing to an end. In 1616, after two exhaustive voyages to the Arctic regions of Canada, William Baffin concluded that there was 'neither passage, nor hope of passage' and most contemporaries accepted his verdict. Hudson had lost his life in a vain quest, which is not to say that his enterprise was fruitless: the river, strait and bay named for him bear witness to his achievement.

Bermuda was colonized by the English in 1612. It is labeled on this map and the next, but not thereafter. The same era saw the establishment of the first permanent habitation in Newfoundland, the English settlement at Cupid's Cove.

Hudson Bay

Henry Hudson
1610–11

James Bay

MONTAGNAIS

Cupid's Cove
(English)

ALGONKIN

Quebec
(French)

Ste Croix

ACADIA
Port Royal
(Fr)

Lake Huron

HURON

Lake Champlain

Lake Ontario

IROQUOIS

Bay of Fundy

Hudson river

Susquehanna

Chesapeake Bay

Henry Hudson
1609

Jamestown
(English)

Bermuda
(English)

St Augustine (Spanish)

NEW MEXICO

Rio Grande

NEW VIZCAYA

NEW LEON

NEW GALICIA

NEW SPAIN

YUCATAN

CUBA

JAMAICA

HISPANIOLA

PUERTO RICO

GUATEMALA

AD
1615

The second English colony in North America was established in 1620 when a group of 100 settlers arrived in Massachusetts Bay aboard the *Mayflower*. The settlers were Puritans, hard-line Protestants who were dissatisfied with the pace of development in the English Church. This particular group, known to history as the Pilgrim Fathers, were prepared to face exile if this meant they could live by their own rules.

The Pilgrim Fathers' original plan was to settle somewhere in the region of the Hudson River. With this in mind they obtained a license from the Virginia Company whose grant covered this area. However, the *Mayflower* arrived off the American coast so late in the season that her captain was not prepared to risk the passage round Cape Cod. The Pilgrims accepted his decision and put ashore at Plymouth. The next spring the fifty of them who were still alive began the hard task of establishing a farming community in the country that was already being referred to as New England.

This term was the invention of a company, the Council for New England, to which the English Crown had entrusted the development of the coastline north of the Hudson. The Pilgrims applied to the Council for a retrospective license, the council was pleased to oblige and, with reinforcements, the Plymouth colony just about managed to keep its head above water through the 1620s. By 1628 there were about 200 people in the colony and 100 more in the rest of New England. The other settlements were at Naumkeag (Salem) and Dover. Naumkeag sheltered perhaps fifty people, the remnants of a disastrous attempt by the council to establish a colony on Cape Ann. Dover, with some twenty-five souls, lay further north, on the stretch of coastline recently christened New Hampshire. And scattered along the New England littoral between these settlements were a couple of dozen fur traders living either in official trading-posts or as individuals fending for themselves. The last group had the best of it, for it was easier to live Indian-style than pioneer a European type of habitation. To the lean and hungry Pilgrims the affluence of these traders was almost as much of an affront as their drinking bouts and Indian girl-friends.

If the English were making slow work of New England, they were still doing better than the French, for whom the 1620s were to be a deeply disappointing decade. The settlement at Port Royal was abandoned in 1623: in 1627 its site was occupied by a Scots expedition which built a fort there and then announced its claim to sovereignty over all Acadia under the title of Nova Scotia (New Scotland). To Champlain's chagrin the French of La Tour Harbor, the only active post in the peninsula, threw in with the Scots. Worse was to come. In 1629 an English privateer forced the surrender of Quebec. Champlain and the 100-odd Québécois who constituted the population of New France had to choose between repatriation and English rule. For Champlain at least, this was no choice at all, and by 1630 he was back in Paris, his dream of empire shattered.

The Virginia colony also had a stormy passage in the 1620s. In 1622 the local Indians made a concerted surprise attack aimed at wiping out the colony. In the case of the more isolated plantations they came perilously close to success; by the time the settlers rallied and drove off their assailants, 347 people, a fifth of the entire population, had been massacred. The overall population figure is from a census taken two years later which provided further cause for alarm, for it showed a total of only 1,275 people in the whole colony. Considering that at least 6,000 Englishmen had landed in Virginia over the preceding seventeen years, this suggested that would-be settlers had only a one in five chance of surviving long enough to enjoy the trumpeted benefits of the New World. 'What has become of the 5,000 missing subjects of His Majesty?' asked a Royal Commission set up to enquire into the Virginia Company's affairs and, getting no good answer, it recommended that the company be dissolved. Virginia became a Crown colony with a royal governor, who called for yet another fresh start. He was rewarded with a marked upturn in the settlement's affairs. The Indians had shot their bolt. Tobacco, the financial mainstay of the colony since its introduction in 1613, was selling well. By 1628 the James Peninsula was firmly in the hands of the settlers.

The years that saw New England begun and Virginia established also witnessed the start of another English colonial enterprise, this time in the Caribbean. The first settlement was made on St Kitts (in 1624, in partnership with a French group that happened to be in the area at the same time), the second and most important on Barbados (in 1627) and the third on Nevis (in 1628, by extension from St Kitts). Barbados had previously been uninhabited: the Caribs on St Kitts and Nevis were soon displaced. The colonists on these lush islands had an easier start of it than their compatriots on the main.

These various advances testify to England's maritime energy during the period under survey. To contemporaries, however, the wonder of the age was not England but Holland. The Dutch Republic was born out of war with Spain, and the Hollanders pursued their quarrel with the Iberian powers (Spain and Portugal were dynastically allied at this time) around the world. Their chosen instrument in the Atlantic was the West India Company (WIC), founded in 1621 with the aim of taking over as much of the traffic between Old World and New as possible. In this aim it was remarkably successful. WIC wrested the slave and sugar trades from the Portuguese. It obtained a stake in the North American fur trade by establishing posts on the Hudson – most importantly Fort Orange (Albany) and New Amsterdam (New York). It also hit the jackpot that so many had tried for but failed to win, the capture of the fleet that carried the year's silver output to Spain. In 1628 Admiral Piet Hein intercepted the convoy as it was entering the Florida Straits, drove it into Matanzas Bay, Cuba, and took enough silver from the grounded galleons to enable WIC to pay its shareholders a 75 percent dividend.[1]

1 For note see p. 106.

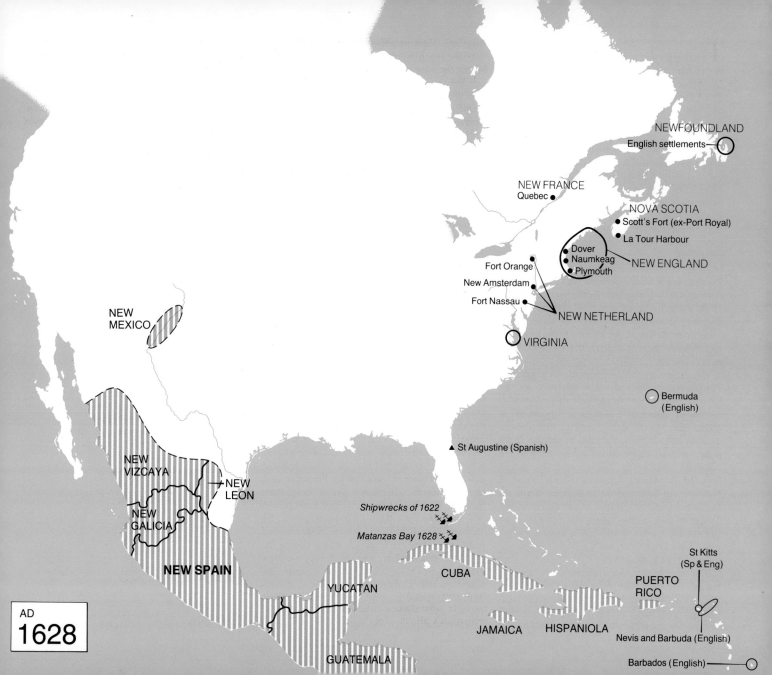

NEWFOUNDLAND
English settlements

NEW FRANCE
Quebec ●

NOVA SCOTIA
● Scott's Fort (ex-Port Royal)
● La Tour Harbour

NEW ENGLAND
● Dover
● Naumkeag
● Plymouth

Fort Orange ●
New Amsterdam ●
Fort Nassau ●
NEW NETHERLAND

NEW MEXICO

VIRGINIA

Bermuda
(English)

St Augustine (Spanish)

NEW VIZCAYA

NEW LEON

NEW GALICIA

NEW SPAIN

YUCATAN

Shipwrecks of 1622

Matanzas Bay 1628

CUBA

JAMAICA

HISPANIOLA

PUERTO RICO

St Kitts
(Sp & Eng)

Nevis and Barbuda (English)

Barbados (English)

GUATEMALA

AD
1628

Towards the end of the 1620s many of the leaders of the Puritan movement in England came to the conclusion that the Pilgrim Fathers had been right. The Church of England was incorrigible and the only way to create a Godly state was to build a new one. They gained control of the Massachusetts Bay Company, an offshoot of the Council for New England, sent an advance party to take over Naumkeag (now renamed Salem) and followed this up the next year by despatching a much larger group which founded the city of Boston (1630). Then they began the transfer of whole communities from Old England to New.

The operations of the Massachusetts Bay Company stand in welcome contrast to earlier endeavors. Where previous colonial ventures had been under-researched and under-capitalized, the Puritans knew what they were doing and had the resources to do it properly. By the beginning of the 1640s when the 'great migration' came to an end, they had transplanted a society of some 10,000 souls from one side of the Atlantic to the other and established it there so securely that its survival was never in doubt.

The expansion of New England was rapid. The Puritan leadership had a low tolerance for the splinter groups that the movement, consisting as it did of committed dissenters, produced in abundance. The dissidents found it politic to move to areas outside the jurisdiction of the Bay Company, and this factor added extra energy to the colonial process. In 1636 breakaway groups founded Providence, opposite Rhode Island in Narragansett Bay, and the three 'river towns' on the Connecticut: the nuclei of two future states. Two years later another colony was established just beyond the Connecticut when a London clergyman, John Davenport, led a group of his parishioners ashore at New Haven.[1]

The other North American colonies were prospering too. The Dutch West India Company had decided to encourage settlers to come to the Hudson valley and had succeeded in attracting enough to bring the population of New Netherland up to a thousand. Their neighbors on the Delaware side were the few hundred Swedes and Finns brought out by the New Sweden Company from 1637 on. To the south lay the English colonies of Chesapeake Bay, Virginia and its companion, Maryland. Virginia was now over its time of troubles and had developed into a community of 8,000 souls. Maryland, granted to Lord Baltimore by King Charles I in 1632, had the relatively easy beginnings characteristic of second-generation colonies and already contained some 1,500 inhabitants. Ostensibly named in honor of Charles's Queen Henrietta Maria, Maryland's hidden dedication was to the Roman faith. The Catholic Lord Baltimore intended it as a refuge for his co-religionists who, like the Puritans, had to endure persecution by the middle-of-the-road Church of England.

Building up every bit as fast as the mainland colonies were the English settlements in the Lesser Antilles. The pace-setter here was undoubtedly Barbados where the population is thought to have grown from 1,000 to 10,000 within a decade. In the Leewards, counting the Anglo-French colony of St Kitts as well as such entirely English additions as Antigua and Montserrat, the increase was from 1,000 to 5,000. The French made their main effort in the larger islands, starting settlements on both Guadeloupe and Martinique (1635). They also ventured into the Greater Antilles at this time, seizing the islet of Tortuga, off Hispaniola, in 1639.

Anglo-French rivalry was muted during these years. King Charles had married a French queen and his main concern was to get the French to keep up the payments on her dowry. To encourage them in this he agreed to return New France and Acadia to French control (1632). Champlain, now in his sixty-sixth year, sailed back to Quebec and managed to breathe some life into it during the time that remained to him. However, the New France to which he had dedicated himself contained less than a hundred people in the year of his death (1635) and no more than 300 in the early 1640s. Acadia was even more sparsely inhabited.

Where the French did make progress was in exploration. In 1634 Jean Nicolet made a memorable voyage through the Great Lakes in the course of which he reached the far side of Lake Huron and discovered both of the major waterways leading into it, the Sault Ste Marie, which he probed but did not traverse, and the Straits of Mackinaw, which led him to Lake Michigan. In the region of Green Bay he came into contact with the Winnebago Indians, the first of the Siouan-speaking tribes to be encountered by a European. What he made of his geographical discoveries no one knows, though it is unlikely that he could make much sense of them when he had no certain knowledge as to how Lakes Huron and Ontario were linked, or indeed whether they were connected at all.

1 The New Hampshire and Maine coasts, which were in theory the subject of separate grants, were effectively absorbed by the Massachusetts Bay Company at this time. The annexations were welcomed by the people on the spot, who needed all the back-up they could get, but were never officially ratified by the English government.

NEWFOUNDLAND

English settlements

Sault Ste Marie

NEW
FRANCE

*Green Bay,
Lake Michigan*

*Lake
Huron*

ACADIA
(French)

Straits of Mackinaw

Lake Ontario

NEW ENGLAND

1
2
3
4
5

1 Massachusetts   4 Connecticut
2 Plymouth   5 New Haven
3 Providence

NEW SWEDEN

NEW NETHERLAND

MARYLAND

VIRGINIA

NEW
MEXICO

St Augustine (Spanish)

NEW
VIZCAYA

NEW LEON

NEW
GALICIA

NEW SPAIN

YUCATAN

CUBA

Tortuga (Fr)

PUERTO
RICO

LESSER ANTILLES

St Kitts   English
(Fr & Eng)   Leewards

JAMAICA

HISPANIOLA

Guadeloupe (Fr)

Martinique (Fr)

GUATEMALA

Barbados (English)

AD
1641

In the middle decades of the seventeenth century the English and French settlers in the Antilles went over to sugar production in a big way. The plantation system they used had been developed by the Portuguese in Brazil. The Dutch introduced it to the Caribbean and provided would-be planters with its two essential ingredients, a supply of black slaves and a guaranteed market for the sugar. The social consequences of the new technology were dramatic. Barbados, one of the first islands to become a significant sugar producer, had an all-white population of 10,000 in 1640: thirty-five years later it had 50,000 people, of whom two-thirds were black.

The huge profits that the Dutch reaped from the slave and sugar trades were, as these things go, fairly earned: no one could match them in terms of efficiency. However, letting the Hollanders take money out of English colonies was not an idea that went down well in London and in 1651 Parliament passed legislation which gave English ship-owners a monopoly of the traffic. The measure precipitated a series of Anglo-Dutch naval wars that lasted, with intermissions, until 1674. Ultimately the contest went England's way. This was not because the Dutch did not have their share of victories – they did, and more – but because the Dutch could not afford to tie up their shipping in long, attritional struggles of this type. Consequently, command of the sea came to rest with England's Royal Navy, and the continuing growth of the English colonial empire, bolstered by the capture of Jamaica from the Spanish (1655) and of New Netherland from the Dutch (1665), was matched by an increase in the maritime power available for its further extension.

New Netherland was acquired by King Charles II during the second Anglo-Dutch war. He gave it to his brother, the Duke of York, in whose honor it was renamed New York. The duke in his turn gave a slice of his winnings, the area east of the Delaware, to his cronies Sir George Carteret and John, Lord Berkeley. Their holdings became known as east and west New Jersey. As the Dutch had absorbed New Sweden into New Netherland back in 1655, there was now a complete line of English colonies running all the way from Massachusetts to Virginia.[1] King Charles extended this line to the south by chartering a new colony named Carolina in 1663. Some settlements were already in existence at the northern end of this stretch of coast (round Albermarle Sound, the nucleus of the future state of North Carolina); a second focus was created in 1670 by the foundation of Charles Town (present-day Charleston).

New France, after a very shaky period in the 1640s, emerged as a viable colony in the 1660s. Most of the difficulties were due to the Iroquois who, in a devastating series of raids along and across the St Lawrence, inflicted grievous losses on the colonists and all but annihilated France's Indian allies, the Algonkin and Huron. For a while all the French could do was keep close to their stockades at Quebec and Montreal (the latter founded in 1642) and hope that if they were caught in the open by an Iroquois raiding-party they would find a quick death in battle rather than have to face the protracted torments that were an Iroquois speciality. Then, in the 1660s, the tide began to turn. The Indian assault ebbed; the arrival of new settlers restored the morale and rebuilt the strength of the colony. When Governor Frontenac took office in 1672, New France had a population of over 5,000 and was able to sustain the forward policy that he initiated.

If the health of New France was improving, so was French comprehension of North America's geography. This was largely because of the activities of the *coureurs de bois*, the traders and trappers whose search for furs carried them ever further into the continent. One of the most important advances was achieved by Medard Chouart, Sieur des Groseilliers, who in 1660 made an epic voyage through the Lake Superior–Hudson Bay region. However, Groseilliers then blotted his patriotic copybook by going to England to get the backing he needed to open up the area. His venture, which involved sailing directly to Hudson Bay, succeeded so brilliantly that in 1670 the London-based Hudson's Bay Company was formed to continue the good work. What had started out as a bit of French enterprise had ended up to the advantage of the English.

Never mind, there was greater glory to be won elsewhere. In 1673 two Frenchmen, Louis Joliet and Father Jacques Marquette, set out from Green Bay, Lake Michigan, on the journey of the century. At the age of twenty-eight Louis Joliet was already a seasoned explorer with the discovery of the connection between Lakes Huron and Erie to his credit. Father Marquette, his senior by seven years, was responsible for setting up and running the Jesuit mission on the Sault Ste Marie (founded 1668). The two of them had heard the local Indians talk of a great river to the west of Lake Michigan which, if it existed, obviously formed part of a different watershed. They decided to go and look for it.

It was early June when Joliet and Marquette crossed the divide between the Fox and Wisconsin rivers. Ten days later they reached the Mississippi. Letting the current carry them downstream they traveled past the mouths of the Missouri, Ohio and Arkansas rivers. Then, confident that the Mississippi could be headed nowhere but the Gulf of Mexico (and not, as Marquette had initially been inclined to believe, for the Pacific) they turned back. By September they were once again at Green Bay, having covered 2,500 miles in four months.

In 1666, at their second attempt, the English succeeded in colonizing the Bahamas.

1 To the number of nine, New Haven having been absorbed by Connecticut in 1664.

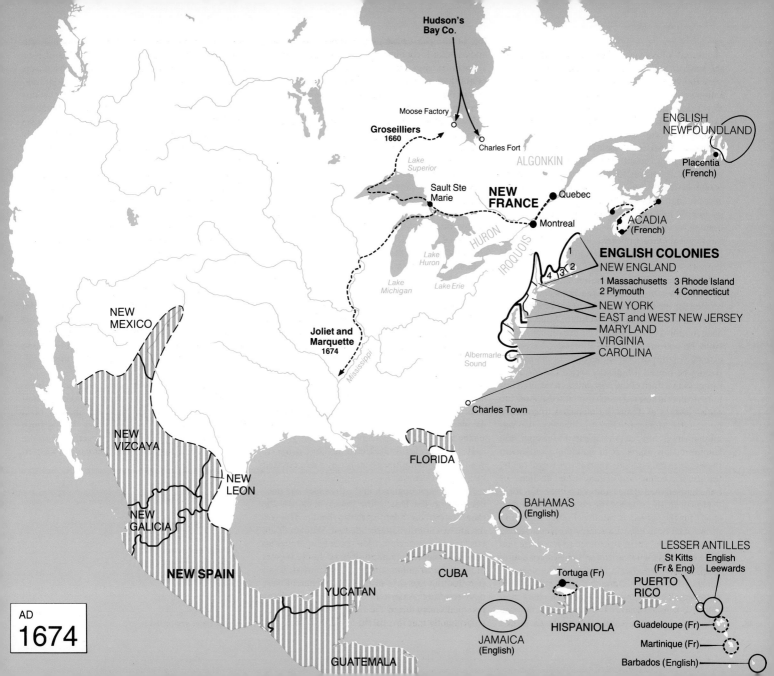

Hudson's Bay Co.

Moose Factory

Groseilliers
1660

Charles Fort

Lake Superior

ALGONKIN

Sault Ste Marie

NEW FRANCE

Quebec

Montreal

HURON

Lake Huron

Lake Michigan

Lake Erie

IROQUOIS

ENGLISH NEWFOUNDLAND

Placentia (French)

ACADIA (French)

ENGLISH COLONIES

NEW ENGLAND

1 Massachusetts   3 Rhode Island
2 Plymouth   4 Connecticut

NEW YORK
EAST and WEST NEW JERSEY
MARYLAND
VIRGINIA
CAROLINA

Albermarle Sound

Joliet and
Marquette
1674

Mississippi

Charles Town

NEW MEXICO

NEW VIZCAYA

NEW LEON

NEW GALICIA

NEW SPAIN

YUCATAN

GUATEMALA

FLORIDA

BAHAMAS (English)

CUBA

Tortuga (Fr)

JAMAICA (English)

HISPANIOLA

PUERTO RICO

LESSER ANTILLES

St Kitts (Fr & Eng)   English Leewards

Guadeloupe (Fr)

Martinique (Fr)

Barbados (English)

AD
1674

The task of converting the French discovery of the Mississippi into a formal claim to sovereignty over the American west was undertaken by La Salle, a young French nobleman who arrived in New France in 1666. A faithful copy of his master, Louis XIV, La Salle was relentless in his pursuit of greatness. Neither technical problems, of which he had a poor grasp, nor ill luck, of which he had more than his share, could divert him from his life's ambition, which was to make France the leading power in North America. With this in mind he descended the Mississippi and, at a ceremony near its mouth in 1682, formally annexed the lands drained by the river and its tributaries. He named the new province Louisiana in honor of the Sun King, to whose court he then returned to lobby for support.

Louis was sufficiently flattered by La Salle's gesture to see he was given the ships and men he needed for the next stage of his plan, which was to establish a settlement on the Gulf of Mexico on or near the Mississippi Delta. The expedition set sail from France in 1684. Unfortunately, La Salle's estimate of the position of the Mississippi was quite wrong: he placed it half way across the continent rather than a third of the way, and as a result of this miscalculation steered much too far west. Arriving on the shores of Texas, he managed to convince himself that Matagorda Bay fitted the little that was known about the outlet of the Mississippi and committed his followers to building a settlement there. Over the next few years it was wiped out by the usual combination of illness and Indians. La Salle himself died at the hand of a mutineer in 1687.

However, this was not the end of the Louisiana story, for the success of another French enterprise in the Americas gave La Salle's project a second chance. In 1697 Spain was forced to recognize that the French had won control of the western half of Hispaniola (thereafter known as St Domingue in contrast to Santo Domingo, the still-Spanish eastern half). Subsequently, one of France's most effective colonial warriors, Pierre d'Iberville, was able to lead a new expedition to Louisiana, build a fort on the coast near present-day Biloxi (1699), and another forty miles up the Mississippi (1700). D'Iberville also made contact with the posts established further up the river by the *coureurs de bois* operating from New France. At last Louisiana was something more than a name on a map.[1]

The English had no equivalent advance to report. The energies of the New England colonies were absorbed first by a debilitating struggle with the local Indians, and then, in the 80s, by a contest with the Crown as to their form of government. As was usual in the seventeenth century, the political problem was expressed in religious terms. The Crown was not prepared to have colonial governments discriminating against members of the Church of England, while colonies such as Massachusetts, which were still controlled by Puritan elders, were determined to weight the scales in favor of the Godly. Of the two contestants the Crown proved the stronger. Massachusetts had its charter cancelled and, along with the rest of the northern colonies, was incorporated in a 'Dominion of New England', ruled by a governor sent out from London. The Dominion did not survive the overthrow of King James II, whose idea it had been, but though his successor, William III, who took an opposite line to James on most questions, restored the majority of the individual colonial governments, he gave them constitutions in the prevailing English mode. The new charters allowed for a considerable measure of self-government (with an electorate determined by a property qualification) but ultimate authority was exercised by a royal governor.[2]

Beyond New England, in the area that had once belonged to the Dutch, the major news was the foundation of the colony of Pennsylvania. This was the life work of the Quaker idealist, William Penn. His guiding principle, his belief in religious freedom, stands in marked contrast to the bigotry of the colonial fathers of the earlier period: it is a sign that the first rays of the Enlightenment were now reaching America's shores. In 1682 Penn personally supervised the laying out of Philadelphia, his 'city of brotherly love': he lived long enough to see it become the second largest in North America (just behind Boston, just ahead of New York). For much of this period Delaware was accounted an appendage of Pennsylvania. However, there were doubts about its exact status because, despite being included in Penn's original grant, it was for some reason not mentioned in his official charter. The uncertainty was eventually resolved when Delaware obtained its own legislature (1704) and executive (1710).

The division of colonial authority in English North America as compared to the totalitarian structure of New France perhaps goes some way towards explaining the relatively poor performance of the English in the war of 1688–97. Another factor was the continuing decline of the Iroquois, England's allies in the land war. The French mounted successful raids into upstate New York, New Hampshire and, in alliance with the Abnaki Indians, Maine. The English proved unable to make an effective riposte. At sea the English did better, but though, as expected, they took Port Royal, they failed in an attempted coup against Quebec. Then everyone went back to the starting line and there was a four-year break in the hostilities before the next round began.[3]

Patient work by dedicated missionaries brought the northern part of Florida and the southern half of peninsular California into the Spanish orbit during the later seventeenth century. The Spanish authorities, nettled by La Salle's activities in the Gulf, put a garrison ashore at Pensacola in western Florida in 1696.[4]

1 For notes see p. 106.

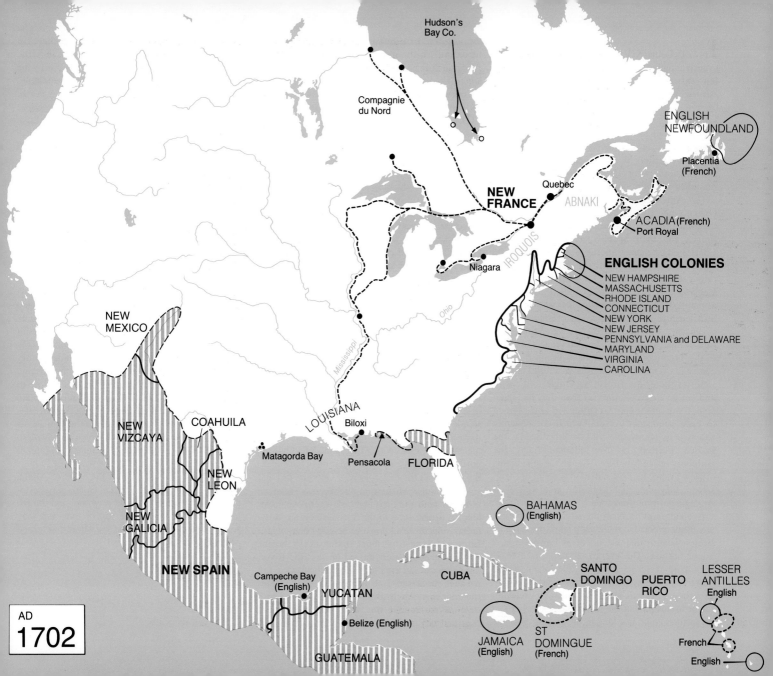

Hudson's Bay Co.

Compagnie du Nord

ENGLISH NEWFOUNDLAND

Placentia (French)

NEW FRANCE

Quebec

ABNAKI

ACADIA (French)
Port Royal

Niagara

IROQUOIS

Ohio

ENGLISH COLONIES
NEW HAMPSHIRE
MASSACHUSETTS
RHODE ISLAND
CONNECTICUT
NEW YORK
NEW JERSEY
PENNSYLVANIA and DELAWARE
MARYLAND
VIRGINIA
CAROLINA

NEW MEXICO

NEW VIZCAYA

COAHUILA

NEW LEON

Mississippi

LOUISIANA

Biloxi

Matagorda Bay

Pensacola

FLORIDA

NEW GALICIA

NEW SPAIN

Campeche Bay (English)

YUCATAN

Belize (English)

GUATEMALA

BAHAMAS (English)

CUBA

SANTO DOMINGO

PUERTO RICO

LESSER ANTILLES
English

JAMAICA (English)

ST DOMINGUE (French)

French

English

AD 1702

In 1702 Louis XIV launched the last and most bitterly fought of all his European aggressions, the ten-year struggle with England, Holland and Austria known as the War of the Spanish Succession. It was not a success. By the time the various belligerents had come to terms, which they eventually did in 1713 in the Treaty of Utrecht, France's armies had been defeated on every important battlefield, its exchequer was bankrupt and its people were starving. Louis was forced to renounce his ambitions for good and all.

The American end of this conflict, known as Queen Anne's War after the English monarch of the time, produced few memorable hostilities. The French and their Spanish allies failed to take Charleston (the contemporary and final spelling of Charles Town). The British – call them British rather than English after 1707 when the crowns of England and Scotland were united – failed in attempts on Quebec and on the Spanish outposts of St Augustine and Pensacola. The only coup of any significance was an expected one, the British capture of Port Royal in Acadia. However, the terms of the Treaty of Utrecht were determined by the course of events in Europe and, as a result of their victories there, the British were able to demand and get far more of America than they had been able to win on the spot. A chastened Louis agreed to cede peninsular Acadia, which consequently resumed its alternative title of Nova Scotia, the French portion of Newfoundland and the periphery of Hudson Bay. Though the inhabitants of New France had given a good account of themselves, they emerged from the war with their strategic position weakened.[1]

In an attempt to repair this situation the French government decided to develop Isle Royale (Cape Breton Island) in the Gulf of St Lawrence as a major bastion. The French colonists from Newfoundland were resettled on the island and a putatively impregnable fortress constructed at Louisbourg. It was all to no avail. The relevant factor in this part of the world was sea power and no fortress could last long in the Gulf without the support of a fleet. In the next round of hostilities between British and French, the War of the Austrian Succession or, in American terminology, King George's War, a combined operation by the British navy and the New England militia took out the fortress after a siege of less than seven weeks.

The War of the Austrian Succession ran from 1740 to 1748. Aside from the capture of Louisbourg (1745), nothing of much moment occurred in North America and if the peace treaty that ended the war had been drawn up locally it would undoubtedly have left the British masters of Isle Royale. But once again, the bottom line was determined by events in Europe. There the French had done well enough to obtain the restitution of Louisbourg. The fact that it had done little to justify its cost did not stop them from spending even more money elaborating and extending its fortifications.

The French were also active in the American south and west. The founding of New Orleans in 1718 provided Louisiana with the administrative center it needed: a line of forts and missions strung along the Mississippi gave some substance to French claims to sovereignty over the whole area. Attempts to extend the boundaries of Louisiana eastward had less success. They turned on the relationship with the Creek Indians, who tended to be more impressed by the British. This was understandable as the most notable events in the area were the British raids of 1703–4, which destroyed the chain of missions that the Spanish had built in northern Florida, and the foundation of Savannah, the nucleus of the new colony of Georgia, in 1733.

West of the Mississippi the French faced an unknown land and their first task was to explore it. Hoping to find ways to the Spanish frontier settlements, which were known to be good markets for European goods, or, more optimistically, to the Pacific, French traders moved up the Red River, the Arkansas and the Platte. The difficulty was not so much the distances as the attitude of the plains Indians, particularly the Apache who lived in a state of permanent war with the Spanish and regarded all Europeans with the utmost suspicion. Eventually a party led by the Mallet brothers got through to Santa Fe from the north, but the dangers of the journey and a frosty reception by the Spaniards made it an effort not worth repeating. French enterprise, both here and in the far north, where, by the exertions of the La Verendrye family, the line of outposts was extended to Lake Winnipeg, petered out well short of the Rockies.

The westward probings of the French prompted the Spaniards to make another attempt to bring Texas within their empire. This time they were successful. A series of permanent posts was established in 1716–17 and ten years later the territory was given formal status as a province (1728). Twenty years after that the Spanish authorities did the same for the Gulf coast to the south of the Rio Grande, a sector which they had previously neglected to occupy: it became the province of New Santander (1747). A third new province, Sinaloa, was erected on the equally barren west coast where the frontier had been edged forward over the previous hundred years, mainly through the missionary activities of the Jesuit fathers.

The second quarter of the eighteenth century saw a start made on the exploration of the extreme north-west of the American continent. Previous to the voyages of Vitus Bering, a Danish captain sailing in Russian service, nothing was known of its geography. It remained a blank on the map and as such was used by the satirist Jonathan Swift to accommodate Brobdingnag, his imaginary land of giants, as late as 1726. Bering's voyage of 1740–1, during which he visited both the coast of Alaska and the islands of the Aleutian chain, gave cartographers something definite to go on, and though his discoveries lie off the top of our map they suggested a line for the coast as a whole that turned out to be substantially correct.

1 For note see p. 106.

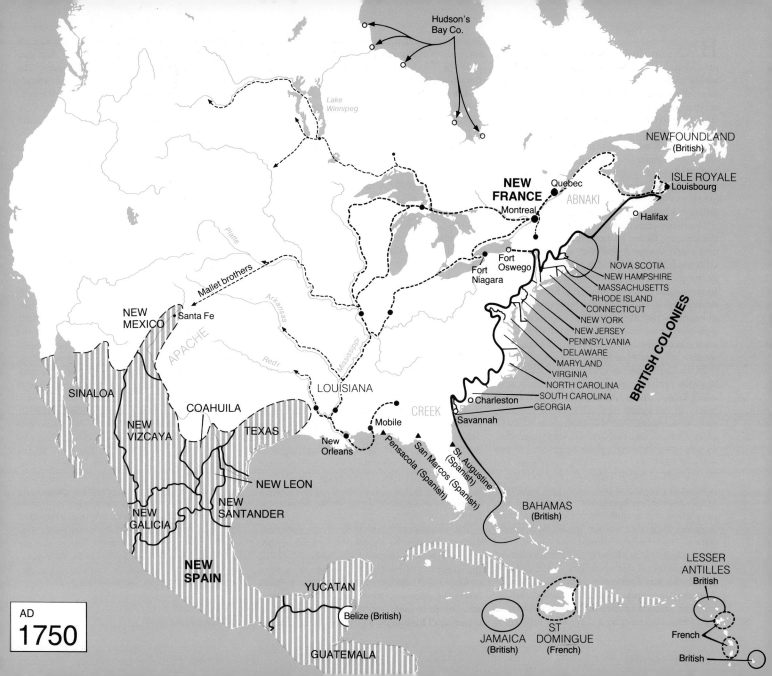

Hudson's
Bay Co.

*Lake
Winnipeg*

Platte

NEW
MEXICO • Santa Fe

APACHE

Arkansas

Mallet brothers

Mississippi

Red r

LOUISIANA

CREEK

SINALOA

NEW
VIZCAYA

COAHUILA

TEXAS

NEW LEON

NEW
GALICIA

NEW
SANTANDER

NEW
SPAIN

New
Orleans

Mobile

Pensacola (Spanish)

San Marcos (Spanish)

St. Augustine (Spanish)

BAHAMAS
(British)

NEW
FRANCE

Quebec

Montreal

ABNAKI

NEWFOUNDLAND
(British)

ISLE ROYALE
Louisbourg

Halifax

Fort
Oswego

Fort
Niagara

NOVA SCOTIA
NEW HAMPSHIRE
MASSACHUSETTS
RHODE ISLAND
CONNECTICUT
NEW YORK
NEW JERSEY
PENNSYLVANIA
DELAWARE
MARYLAND
VIRGINIA
NORTH CAROLINA
SOUTH CAROLINA
GEORGIA

BRITISH
COLONIES

Charleston

Savannah

YUCATAN

Belize (British)

GUATEMALA

JAMAICA
(British)

ST
DOMINGUE
(French)

LESSER
ANTILLES
British

French

British

AD
1750

Between the close of the fifteenth century, the date when we last had a population map, and the middle of the eighteenth century, the date of this one, the number of people in North America went up modestly. The tally adopted here gives a rise from 6.5 million to 8.5 million and an increment of 2 million, or 30 percent. The area's population history was, however, rather more interesting than this bare statement would suggest, for in the first half of the period numbers actually fell by 1.5 million, which means that the rising phase of the graph was that much steeper, with a gain of 3.5 million on 5 million, or 66 percent.

The major centers of Amerindian population in the southern half of Mexico and the northern half of Central America rode out this demographic switchback fairly comfortably. Though the number of people of pure Indian stock was probably somewhat lower in 1750 than it had been in 1500, it is likely that the difference was made up by immigrants and mixed-bloods. This is the view presented on the map which reckons the Indians at 80 percent of the 1492 figure and the Spanish and mestizo populations at 10 percent each.

In the Caribbean the changes were much more dramatic. The natives were wiped out and a new, much larger, immigrant population put in their place. In numerical terms 200,000 Amerindians were replaced by 300,000 Europeans and 750,000 black Africans. The economic engine for this transformation was the sugar plantation, with its labor force of black slaves. In 1750 St Domingue, the French half of Santo Domingo, was the biggest producer of sugar and had the largest number of blacks both in absolute terms (200,000) and as a proportion of the whole (90 percent). Next came Jamaica, then the smaller British and French islands. The Spanish possessions – Cuba, the eastern half of Santo Domingo, and Puerto Rico – had populations that were less dense and less black. This was a reflection of the slower pace of economic development in the Spanish sphere.

North America's population had also undergone a profound metamorphosis. In place of the 100,000 Indians who had formed the pre-Columban population of the eastern seaboard, there was a chain of English colonies stretching from Newfoundland to Georgia that contained well over a million people of European or African stock. The two northernmost colonies, Newfoundland and Nova Scotia, hardly count, for they had no more than 6,000 inhabitants each, but the New England colonies could boast a formidable population of 350,000 (Massachusetts 180,000, Connecticut 100,000, Rhode Island 35,000 and New Hampshire 30,000). The middle group, with 300,000, was only marginally less populous (Pennsylvania plus Delaware 150,000, New York 80,000, New Jersey 65,000), while the southern colonies contained as many whites as New England plus almost the entire colonial total of 200,000 black slaves (taking whites and blacks together the figures are Virginia 250,000, the Carolinas 150,000, Maryland 140,000 and Georgia, where settlement had only just started, a mere 5,000). The final total, excluding the geographically detached colonies of Newfoundland and Nova Scotia, amounted to 1.2 million.

It hardly needs saying the creation of this colonial population represents the most important change in direction in American history since the original peopling of the continent. There were now as many white men as red men north of the Rio Grande and whereas Amerindian numbers were declining, the population of the thirteen colonies of the mainland was increasing at a staggering rate. On a conservative estimate it was doubling every twenty-five years, and with good agricultural land in abundant supply there was no reason why it should not continue to do so for the foreseeable future.

The French contribution to North American demography was, by comparison with the British, relatively minor. In essence it consisted of the 50,000 settlers of New France, though there were another 10,000 people of French stock in Nova Scotia and the islands of the Gulf of St Lawrence, and perhaps 4,000 more in the province of Louisiana. The outlook for the smaller groups was clouded. If the English took over, as they already had in Nova Scotia, it seemed likely that they would eventually swamp the French element. The Québecois, on the other hand, had already achieved the numerical strength necessary to preserve their identity come what may.

As far as the Indians are concerned, it is worth stating that as yet only a minority of those north of the Rio Grande had felt the impact of the European immigration. The pueblo Indians had passed under the Spanish yoke, but otherwise the tribes west and north-west of the Mississippi remained untrammelled. The population density was low enough to prevent European diseases spreading, the contact with traders too infrequent to disrupt social patterns. There were even some positive benefits. The Apache and the Navaho and, starting about the date of this map, the nearer of the plains Indians, learned the use of the horse from the Spaniards in New Mexico: the Indians of the Woodland zone acquired iron tools from the English and French. But east of the Mississippi the tribes had less to be thankful for, and east of the Appalachians very little at all. Here the Indians' story was one of dispossession and depopulation. Of the 120,000 who had lived in the area now occupied by the Thirteen Colonies, perhaps 20,000 survived.[1]

What had happened to the missing 100,000 Indians of the eastern seaboard? Nearly all had died, either as a result of the vicious, genocidal wars that punctuated the early history of all the American colonies, or as a result of the epidemic spread of European diseases – most notably smallpox, though tuberculosis perhaps played an equally important role in the longer run. Most Indian tribes were small, with less than a thousand members, and soon reached the point where they simply folded up as social units. Some, like the Delaware, tried to make a new life for themselves west of the Appalachians; the vast majority fought where they stood, lost and dwindled away.

1 For note see p. 106.

1,000,000 ———
100,000 ———

Indian

Mestizo

White

Black

Population in
AD
1750

By the early 1750s the area of conflict between the British and French in North America had widened considerably. Originally the two had only been able to get at each other by sea or round the northern end of the Appalachians. Then the foundation of Georgia and the eastward progress of Louisiana created a new front in the south. Now war was joined across the mountain chain as the French sent teams into the Ohio valley and the Virginians, who claimed the area both by treaty with the Iroquois and by Royal Charter, moved to eject them.

The man entrusted with this delicate task – in the first instance diplomatic, but if all else failed, military – was Major George Washington. In 1753 he paid a visit to the French in the Ohio valley and told them they were trespassing. The French were impressed with Washington personally, for he was a fine figure of a man, 6 feet 2 inches tall, with strong features and a commanding manner. On the other hand, he was only twenty-one years old, his commission was in the Virginia militia, a part-time organization better known for drinking than fighting, and he had no soldiers with him. Politely but firmly the French rejected his warnings: they were staying where they were.

Washington returned home determined to uphold Virginia's claim. He persuaded the governor to promote him to lieutenant-colonel and give him command of the 160 militiamen immediately available. Then he recrossed the mountains and fell on a French detachment manning what he assumed to be an outpost. In fact, it was an embassy and Washington found himself with the dubious distinction of having started a war by firing on a diplomatic mission. Worse still, when the local French commander heard what had happened he took a troop of regulars from Fort Duquesne, surprised Washington's camp and forced his surrender. The young Virginian was released only after he had signed a document admitting his fault.

The main reason for Washington's defeat was that France was a major power and Virginia, on its own, a very minor one. If the American colonists were to be effective they had to band together. This was so obvious that delegates of the seven northern colonies were already meeting at Albany to discuss plans for co-ordinated military action. Eventually they approved a protocol drawn up by Benjamin Franklin of Pennsylvania and Thomas Hutchinson of Massachusetts which called for a Federal command and appropriate financial contributions. This should put a stop to French aggressions and, incidentally, show the government in London that Americans were perfectly able to conduct their own affairs.

Alas, not a single colony ratified the Albany plan. This meant that if the French were to be ejected from the Ohio valley, something that everyone was agreed on, the king's government would have to do the job. Anticipating the failure of the colonial initiative, the authorities in London had already set the machinery in motion. In early 1755 General Braddock and two regiments of foot departed Ireland for Alexandria, Virginia. From there they marched to the upper Ohio. Washington, serving as one of Braddock's aides-de-camp, must have contrasted this splendidly turned-out body of men – red coats, banners and drums – with the ragged militia he had led the same way the year before. This time, though, he was not the only one to be disappointed. As they came up on Fort Duquesne the British were shot to pieces by the French and their Indian allies in a fire-fight that was a larger scale version of the Americans' defeat. With Braddock mortally wounded and most of his officers dead or dying, it was left to Washington to lead the survivors back across the mountains. This he did successfully, which made him just about the only person to emerge from the whole dismal business with credit.

The next year the war became official. Known in Europe as the Seven Years War and in America as the French and Indian War, the contest opened well for the French: they took Fort Oswego, the British outpost on Lake Ontario, the first year, and Fort William Henry, Britain's counter to their Fort Ticonderoga, the next. However, in 1758 William Pitt took over as Britain's prime minister and he gave the imperial war-effort the strategic direction it had hitherto lacked. Where his predecessors had never been clear whether to put Europe or America first, Pitt had no doubt that America was the one to go for. And the way to win in America was to strike at Quebec, the heart of New France.

To prevent the French from concentrating their forces at the center, Pitt directed that pressure be kept up on the periphery. One task force re-occupied Oswego and then went on to take out Fort Frontenac, while another made an unsuccessful attempt on Ticonderoga. A third marched against Fort Duquesne. George Washington, a full colonel now, commanded Virginia's contribution to this expedition, which was matched by a brigade of Pennsylvanians and rounded out by a regiment of the British Army. Rendered cautious by experience, Washington rated the chances of success at no better than fifty-fifty, but he was too near the ground to see the grand strategy. For while these subsidiary campaigns were still in progress, Pitt had cleared the way to Quebec. In July 1758 two British brigades landed on Cape Breton Island and forced the surrender of Louisbourg, leaving the French no option but to recall their outlying garrisons. As a result, Washington arrived before Fort Duquesne to find it deserted, an experience he found such a let-down that he decided then and there to resign his commission.

Next year the Royal Navy took General Wolfe and the army that had captured Louisbourg up the St Lawrence to Quebec. For two months Wolfe probed the defenses looking for a weak spot, then, failing to find one, he ordered his men back to their boats and, under cover of darkness, moved them to the heights on the far side of the town. By the time the French came hurrying back to meet him he had his troops drawn up, ready for a demonstration bit of musketry. The French fired the first volley, which was ragged and ineffective. The British reply blew the French ranks apart and sent the survivors tumbling back into Quebec. Four days later the French commander asked for terms.

It took one more campaign to achieve the capture of Montreal, which made its formal submis-

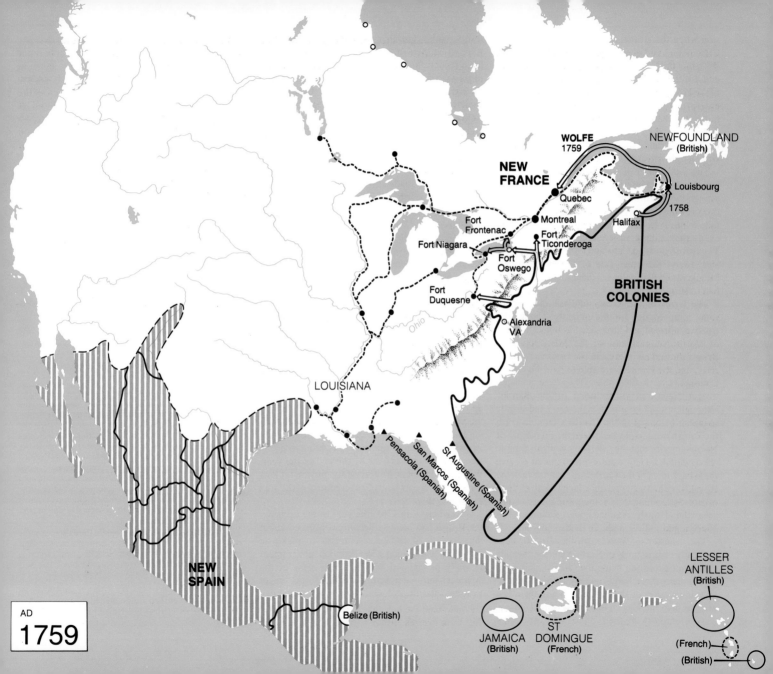

WOLFE
1759

NEWFOUNDLAND
(British)

**NEW
FRANCE**

Quebec

Louisbourg

1758

Montreal

Halifax

Fort
Frontenac

Fort
Ticonderoga

Fort Niagara

Fort
Oswego

**BRITISH
COLONIES**

Fort
Duquesne

Ohio

Alexandria
VA

LOUISIANA

Pensacola (Spanish)

San Marcos (Spanish)

St Augustine (Spanish)

**NEW
SPAIN**

Belize (British)

LESSER
ANTILLES
(British)

JAMAICA
(British)

ST
DOMINGUE
(French)

(French)

(British)

AD
1759

sion when the British forces from Quebec, Lake Champlain and Lake Ontario met under its walls. With that the French dominion in Canada was at an end, for the government in Paris, to the great relief of the French taxpayer, now decided to abandon an enterprise to which its commitment had never been more than half-hearted. When the peace-makers met in 1763, the French had already decided to let both Canada and Louisiana go. The triumph of the British in North America seemed complete.[1]

The final phase of the Seven Years War was enlivened by the intervention of Spain. Burning to avenge the injuries suffered at British hands over the previous 200 years, the Spanish were easily talked into it by the French, but, far from getting even, they simply suffered further humiliation. The British invaded Cuba and took Havana in 1762 and, round the other side of the globe, seized Manila in the Philippines. To get them back Spain had to surrender Florida.[2]

The terms of the Treaty of Paris did contain some compensation for this indignity. Though the treaty confirmed and formalized Britain's mastery of North America east of the Mississippi, the British showed no interest in the lands west of the river, and the French were able to pass this half of Louisiana over to their allies. They even managed to get New Orleans included in the transfer although it was to the east of the river and strictly speaking belonged in the British sector. In truth the British were so pleased to see the French out of North America that they were not going to quibble about details. They were even prepared to give them back most of the Caribbean islands which the Royal Navy had scooped up, which was all of them except St Domingue. Of their conquests in this area the British retained only Dominica, St Vincent and, off the map, Grenada and Tobago.[3]

The transfer of power to the British went smoothly in most parts of North America, the only significant exception being the Great Lakes area. The Indians there had originally formed a favorable impression of the British, finding them less zealous than the French in matters of religion and less peremptory in their diplomacy. And their trade goods were cheaper. But now the British were to be their masters, many Indians began to have second thoughts. The British had, after all, dispossessed and destroyed most of the tribes of the east. Was it not more than likely that they had similar plans for the Indians of the west? As the Redcoats marched in, the chiefs eyed them warily and some young braves openly called for war.

The man who took advantage of this mood to create a wider alliance than any achieved before by an Indian leader was Pontiac, a chieftain of the Ottawa. He persuaded two related tribes, the Ojibway to the north of Lake Superior, and the Potawatomi of present-day Michigan, to join in an offensive against the British which, because it took the form of simultaneous surprise attacks against the various British outposts in the area, is usually referred to as Pontiac's conspiracy. It was not really any more conspiratorial than any other Indian onslaught, infiltration and surprise being standard tactics. The unusual feature was the scale.

Initially Pontiac had considerable success. Eight of the dozen forts in the region fell in quick succession and several additional tribes, most notably the Miami and the Huron, were persuaded to join the alliance. But Forts Detroit, Niagara and Pitt (ex-Duquesne) held out against all attacks and they were the ones that mattered. Pontiac's braves kept up the pressure for a few months, then, following the normal pattern of Indian warfare, began drifting back to their villages. Although the relieving British columns had some sharp fighting to do, in essence the war was over by the end of the year. When Pontiac made his formal submission (at Fort Oswego, two years later) British control of the area was firmer than ever.

Nevertheless, in 1763, the year of the uprising, the British had been sufficiently concerned about the strength of Indian resentment to make an important concession. The London government formally proclaimed that all lands west of the Appalachian watershed constituted an Indian Reserve, that the colonial charters that had been granted 'sea to sea' (i.e., Atlantic to Pacific) did not apply west of this line, and that the Indians, even if they wanted to, could not legally sell any part of this homeland. In theory the only areas open to European settlement lay to the north in Quebec Province (whose westward boundary bisected Lake Ontario) and to the south in the Floridas (whose northern limits were placed at 31°N initially and 32° 30′ in 1764). However, no one doubted that the bar to westward expansion imposed on the colonies by the proclamation of 1763 was temporary and that in the end much of the 'Indian Reserve' was going to end up in white ownership. It was just a matter of waiting for Indian rancors to cool before making the next advance.

1 The British treated the French of Quebec generously. The same cannot be said about their handling of the Acadians, but then the Acadians had come under British rule at a time when the issue of the contest between the two powers was still in doubt. In 1755, after some incidents in which the Acadians failed to observe the neutrality enjoined on them by treaty, the British authorities decided to deport the whole community. Approximately 7,000 individuals (out of a total of 8,000) were rounded up and dispersed among the American colonies. Some of these eventually made their way to French-speaking areas, most notably the group ancestral to the present day Cajuns (i.e. Acadians) of Louisiana.

2 The Spanish also had to recognize the existence of the British settlement at Belize in Central America. This consisted of a few hundred people felling and exporting log wood (a heartwood from which a black dye was extracted) and, later on in the century, mahogany.

3 North of the Mississippi the British frontier is shown following the watershed line granted to the Hudson's Bay Company in its original charter and now no longer in contest.

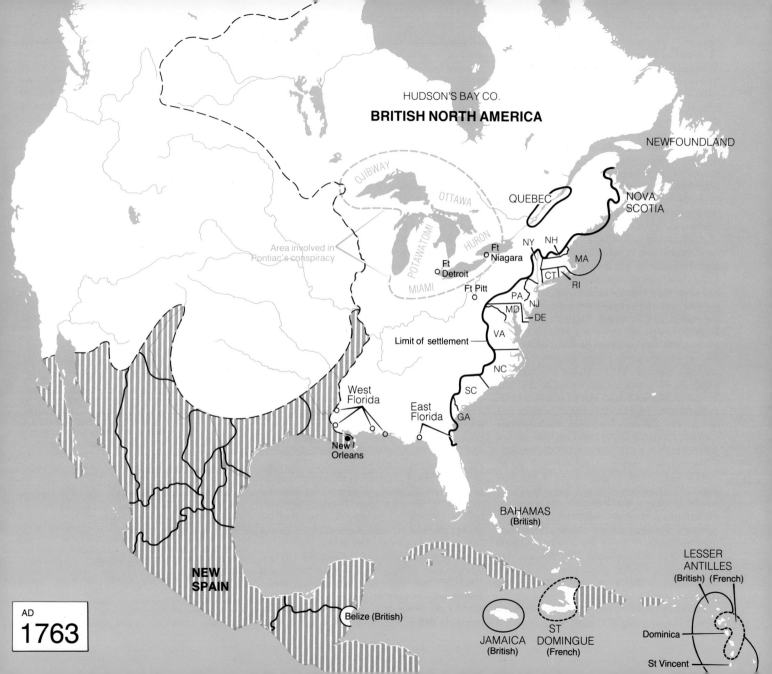

HUDSON'S BAY CO.

BRITISH NORTH AMERICA

NEWFOUNDLAND

QUEBEC

NOVA SCOTIA

OJIBWAY

OTTAWA

POTAWATOMI

HURON

MIAMI

Area involved in
Pontiac's conspiracy

Ft
○ Niagara

Ft
○ Detroit

Ft Pitt
○

NY   NH

MA

CT

RI

PA

MD   NJ

DE

VA

Limit of settlement

NC

SC

West
Florida

East
Florida

GA

●
New
Orleans

**NEW
SPAIN**

Belize (British)

BAHAMAS
(British)

JAMAICA
(British)

ST
DOMINGUE
(French)

LESSER
ANTILLES
(British) (French)

Dominica

St Vincent

AD
1763

The ending of the French threat to British North America caused the British government and the American colonies to look at their relationship anew. The colonies, with their 2 million free citizens, had clearly come of age, but that simple statement was read very differently by the two sides. To the British government it meant the colonies should cease to be a charge on the British taxpayer. A proportion of the sum needed to keep the colonies must in future be raised on the spot. With this in mind, Prime Minister George Grenville decided to tighten up the American customs and impose a stamp duty on all legal transactions (1765). Between them these two measures should have raised £100,000 a year, a not unreasonable contribution considering that the annual expenditure was three times that amount.

The Americans saw the matter differently. They had never been directly taxed before, did not like the idea at all and had good grounds for regarding the stamp duty as illegal. One of the reasons Englishmen were free and most other nations were not was that they could not be taxed without the consent of their elected representatives, specifically the members of the House of Commons sitting in Parliament at Westminster. Yet the American colonies had no elected representatives at Westminster, nor was it practical for them ever to have any. The only conclusion that a patriotic American could draw was that the new British government was attempting to establish a tyranny.

The colonists' mood of outrage built up so quickly and became so general that it was soon clear that the authorities would never be able to enforce the Stamp Act. Bowing to the inevitable, the British government withdrew it and concentrated instead on trying to improve the revenue from the customs (1766–7). These duties were legal but almost equally unpopular, and to protect the custom-houses and their officials the British had to put troops into Boston, the main center for the collection of the customs' dues.

The British had now painted themselves into a corner. The one thing all Englishmen were agreed on was that the Crown should not have at its disposal a standing army of sufficient size to threaten civil liberty. Yet the British were now maintaining an army in Boston which was every bit as offensive to American patriotism. The surprising thing is that when a detachment of British soldiers fired into a mob threatening to loot the Boston Custom-House and five people were killed, the revolution did not erupt immediately. It seems that Sam and John Adams, the organizers of the Patriot Party, deliberately defused the situation because it smacked of lawlessness. What they wanted was a disciplined bit of provocation and, in 1773, in the form of the famous 'Tea Party', they provided it. One hundred and fifty Patriots, lightly disguised as Mohican Indians, took over three ships in Boston harbor and tipped their cargoes of tea, which was dutiable, overboard. The British reacted with the ill-temper that the Adamses had hoped for. Massachusetts was put under a military governor, General Thomas Gage, and the port of Boston closed pending payment of a fine.

General Gage had enough men to control Boston, but nowhere near enough to carry his writ through the countryside. In normal times he could have relied on the help of the local militia, but by now the militia had to be counted as part of the Patriot organization. And if General Gage had any doubts on this score they were settled in April 1775 when 700 Redcoats set out for Concord, a village twenty miles west of Boston, with orders to find and destroy a cache of munitions stockpiled by the Patriots. The expedition was a disaster. There was trouble with the Patriot militia at Lexington on the road to Concord, while at Concord itself there was open battle. Sniped at from all sides, the British column fell back in increasing disorder. Only the prompt despatch of reinforcements from Boston enabled it to regain the safety of the city.

At this point British control over the Thirteen Colonies evaporated. Delegates to the Continental Congress meeting at Philadelphia voted unanimously to support the New Englanders in penning the British army into Boston and, in due course, forcing its evacuation. To direct this enterprise, they nominated Colonel George Washington of the Virginia delegation.

When Washington arrived in the lines before Boston he found the army he was to command in a dispirited state. It had failed to hold a forward position established at Bunker Hill, overlooking the city; it was clearly in no shape to mount a formal assault. Nor could Washington hope to starve the British out: with complete command of the sea they could bring in supplies and reinforcements as they pleased. The answer to the problem was the artillery that had fallen into Patriot hands at Fort Ticonderoga, over on Lake Champlain. Moving the guns took all winter but, in March 1776, they were finally manhandled into positions commanding Boston harbor. The British, who had early on recognized that their position in Boston could easily be rendered untenable in exactly this way, got into their boats and sailed away, never to return. The Thirteen States were free at last.[1]

1 There are three additional points to note on this map. The first is the Patriot invasion of Canada. This was a two-pronged affair with Quebec as its objective. One force advanced on the city via Lake Champlain and Montreal (which fell in late 1775), the other via the Kennebec valley. The second is the appearance of the first trans-Appalachian settlements round Fort Pitt and in Kentucky. The backers of the Kentucky venture hoped to establish a new colony under the name of Transylvania but the settlers who took the Wilderness Trail (marked out for them by Daniel Boone in 1775) saw no need to add to their already frightening degree of isolation and preferred to remain under the protection and authority of Virginia.

The third event is one which at any other period bar this exceptionally busy one would rate a couple of paragraphs in itself. In 1769–70 the Spanish sent a maritime expedition to upper California which established permanent posts at San Diego and Monterey and then went on to make the first recorded exploration of San Francisco Bay. By 1776, when a second expedition arrived via the land route, the number of missions and settlements established in the northern half of the new province (California had been accorded provincial status in 1767) had risen to eight. At the same time Spain resumed her long-abandoned exploration of the north-west, Juan Perez sailing along Vancouver's Pacific coast in 1774 and Bruno Heceta discovering the estuary of the Columbia a year later. Both missed the Strait of Juan de Fuca. All these Spanish moves were precipitated by fear of further advance on the part of the Russian fur traders operating in the Aleutians.

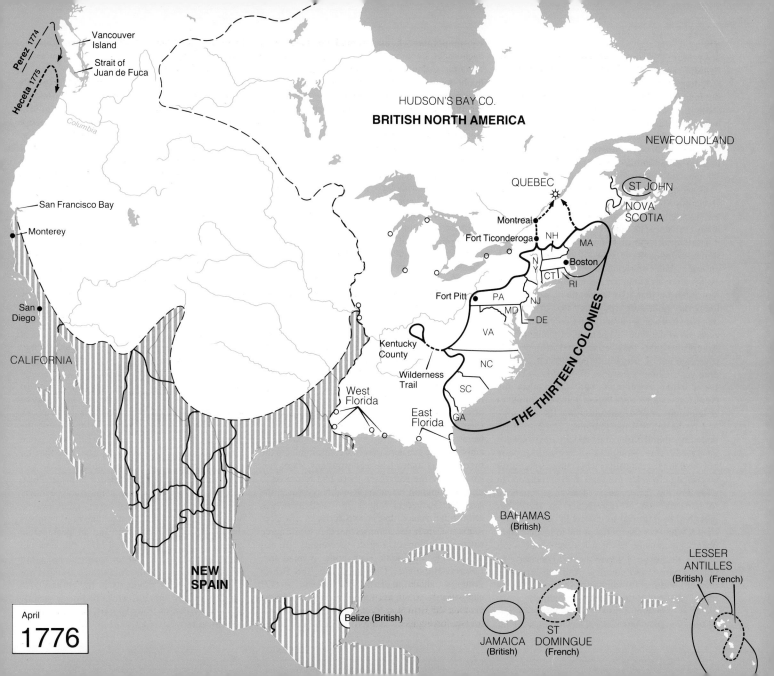

Perez 1774
Heceta 1775

Vancouver
Island

Strait of
Juan de Fuca

Columbia

HUDSON'S BAY CO.

BRITISH NORTH AMERICA

NEWFOUNDLAND

QUEBEC

ST JOHN

NOVA
SCOTIA

Montreal

San Francisco Bay

Monterey

NH

Fort Ticonderoga

MA

N Y

Boston

CT

RI

Fort Pitt

PA

San
Diego

NJ

MD

DE

CALIFORNIA

VA

Kentucky
County

NC

Wilderness
Trail

West
Florida

SC

East
Florida

GA

THE THIRTEEN COLONIES

BAHAMAS
(British)

**NEW
SPAIN**

LESSER
ANTILLES
(British) (French)

Belize (British)

ST
DOMINGUE
(French)

JAMAICA
(British)

April
1776

By May 1776 the Thirteen Colonies and the British Crown had been at war for more than a year but, despite the complete rupture of relations that this implied, the Continental Congress had still not committed itself to a formal declaration of independence. In June, Richard Henry Lee proposed that this unsatisfactory state of affairs be remedied forthwith. Congress responded by setting up a committee and the committee asked Thomas Jefferson of the Virginia delegation to draft an appropriate document. He presented his Declaration to the Congress on 1 July. On the 4th it was adopted and America was able to celebrate, as it has ever since, its official birthday.

The Declaration of Independence has, understandably enough in view of the principles it enshrines, gained a significance that transcends the events that occasioned it. It is, however, worth remembering that it is a document with a contemporary political purpose and that the sections that read less well today may have seemed the most germane at the time. To persuade the majority of Americans that they constituted a new and sovereign nation was surely not difficult. A hundred years earlier a member of the Royal Council for Foreign Plantations had noted that the New Englanders were 'upon the very brink of renouncing any dependence of the Crowne' and in the interval the sentiment in favor of repudiating the British connection can only have increased. But America's new leaders were not seeking a majority, what they were after was unanimity. To this end they produced an all-embracing catalogue of grievances intended to persuade the average American that Congress had been forced to this act in defense of his rights. Whatever the merits of the individual complaints – and some of them had very little merit at all – the list as a whole seemed conclusive to both Congress and country. And it is arguable that in choosing to emphasize the legal aspects of the case rather than simply appealing to sentiment or common sense, the founding fathers of the republic gave the Declaration's better known phrases on life and liberty their safest anchorage.

As the Continental Congress assumed the fine feathers of sovereign government, so the British determined to pluck them. They had never accepted the events in Boston as anything but a temporary, purely tactical defeat, and when General Howe, General Gage's successor in command at Boston, sailed off to the Loyalist haven of Halifax, Nova Scotia, he already had in his pocket orders to occupy New York, together with the promise of an army large enough to enable him to do so. By midsummer all was ready for the planned counter-offensive. In July 1776 Howe sailed from Halifax to Staten Island, New York, with the leading elements of a force that was soon built up to a strength of 20,000 men. In August he drove Washington's army (about the same size as his own) from Long Island. And that was just the beginning. In a humiliating series of reverses Washington lost New York City (September), the rest of Manhattan (October) and the forts on the lower Hudson (November). Finally, in December, Howe sent 6,000 men under General Clinton to occupy Newport, Rhode Island.

The British had, no question of it, forced their way back into the Thirteen Colonies. What they had not done was win over any significant number of the colonists. Their rule extended only as far as their outposts and it was difficult to see how they were going to recover their North American empire with the troops they had committed. On the other hand, Canada had been won back at very low cost – the American force there had retreated to Lake Champlain when the Royal Navy raised the siege of Quebec in May 1776 – and there was always the chance that a bold series of advances might so dismay the colonists that they would agree to a restoration of British sovereignty. It was presumably with some such hope in mind that General Burgoyne, Commander of the British Army in Canada, made his proposal for the 1777 campaign, a march via Lake Champlain and the Hudson valley to New York. With less than 10,000 men he could hardly hope to hold the line of the Hudson but he could bring home to Americans the fact that King George still regarded them as his subjects.

General Howe at New York knew of Burgoyne's plans and was prepared to help him on the last leg of his journey down the Hudson. He also had important plans of his own. In July 1777 he put out to sea with two thirds of his force, reappearing in August at the head of Chesapeake Bay. Washington hastily interposed his army between Howe's force and Philadelphia, but Howe knocked him out of the position he had taken alongside Brandywine Creek and marched his redcoats into Philadelphia. He was now master of the two largest cities in the United States, Philadelphia with its 40,000 inhabitants and New York with its 20,000, and if this did little significant damage to the American cause – the nation's resources were essentially rural – it certainly impaired its dignity.

Meanwhile, Burgoyne was past the halfway mark on his march south from Canada. The 10,000 men with whom he set out had dwindled to 6,000, the pace of his advance had slowed and the size of the American force opposing him, which he had initially outnumbered, was increasing rapidly. At Saratoga the Americans stood and fought, and Burgoyne failed to break through. He couldn't go forward, he wouldn't go back and his situation quickly deteriorated. A month later, beaten back into his camp and outnumbered three to one, he capitulated. The Americans were able to count 5,000 prisoners as evidence of a victory that far outweighed the loss of Philadelphia.

For Howe and the main British army at Philadelphia the winter passed comfortably enough. Washington's men, camped twenty miles away at Valley Forge, had a miserable time of it: numbers dwindled daily as bitter cold and an incompetent commissariat took their toll. But the news of Saratoga had reached Europe and produced a shift of opinion in favor of the American cause that was as important as the victory itself. In February 1778 the French government, which had been secretly aiding the colonists from the start, came out openly on their side.

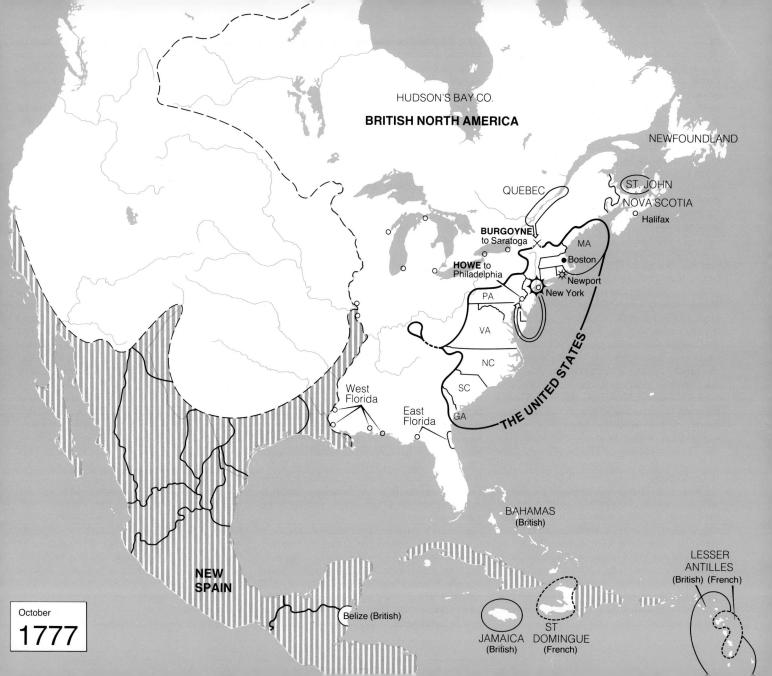

HUDSON'S BAY CO.

BRITISH NORTH AMERICA

NEWFOUNDLAND

QUEBEC

ST. JOHN
NOVA SCOTIA
o Halifax

BURGOYNE
to Saratoga ✕

MA
● Boston

HOWE to
Philadelphia

Newport

New York

PA

VA

NC

SC

GA

THE UNITED STATES

West
Florida

East
Florida

BAHAMAS
(British)

**NEW
SPAIN**

o Belize (British)

JAMAICA
(British)

ST
DOMINGUE
(French)

LESSER
ANTILLES
(British) (French)

October
1777

The news that the French had entered into a formal alliance with the United States forced the British to make fundamental changes in their strategy for the Americas. Troops and ships would have to be redeployed to protect Britain's islands in the Caribbean. The French were bound to attack them and the City of London, which rated the islands more highly than the mainland colonies, insisted that they be given priority. The British cabinet concurred. General Clinton, General Howe's successor in the North American command, was ordered to send 5,000 men to the Caribbean theater even though this meant withdrawing from Philadelphia, the one solid gain of the 1777 campaign.

These dispositions enabled the British to make a very fair showing in 1778. Clinton conducted the retreat from Philadelphia with skill. Washington proved unable to mount an effective attack on the British while they were *en route* to New York and made no attempt to do so once they had reached the safety of the city. The regiments transferred to the Caribbean made their presence felt by taking St Lucia from the French and holding it against a determined counter-attack. This was more than adequate compensation for the loss of Dominica earlier in the year. Most important of all, Clinton regained the initiative in the North American theater with a shrewdly timed blow against Georgia, the southernmost and least steadfast of the Thirteen Colonies. His expeditionary force took Savannah in December and had gained control over the backcountry by early 1779.

The British cabinet was particularly delighted with the news from Georgia because the strength of the Loyalist sentiment uncovered there suggested that the war might be a winnable one after all. According to General Clinton, it would soon be feasible to turn the government of the colony over to the civil arm and place its defense in the hands of the local militia. If true, this would free the regular forces for a move against South Carolina where the Loyalists were said to be equally strong. And so on, step by step, up to New York.

For the first time since the war began the British now had a rational strategy for winning it. Clearly everything depended on the Loyalist element and all one could safely say on this was that it was undoubtedly stronger in the south than the north. But everything that happened in the remaining months of 1779 confirmed the assumptions on which the new strategy was based. Recruiting for Georgia's Loyalist militia went forward at a satisfactory rate, the governor of the colony was able to return from London and resume his official duties, and two Patriot counter-offensives, including one that had the support of a French fleet, were beaten off. The time had come for the next step forward.

By careful marshalling of his resources, in particular by calling in the troops occupying Newport, Clinton was able to put together a formidable task force for the second stage of the plan, the invasion of South Carolina. Taking command of the expedition himself, he sailed from New York at the end of 1779, and by early 1780 had succeeded in bringing Charleston under siege. The city, together with its garrison of 5,000, surrendered in May. It was a stunning defeat, the worst suffered by the Patriot cause so far.

With South Carolina slipping from its grasp, Congress turned to General Horatio Gates, the hero of Saratoga, conferring on him command of all the troops in the southern theater. These amounted to some 3,500 men, rather more than were available to the British commander, General Cornwallis (Clinton had returned to New York). But when battle was joined – at Camden, in August 1781 – it was the British who had the best of it. American strength in the area dipped below the 1,000 mark.

As might be expected, the success of their operations in South Carolina encouraged the British to move against North Carolina. It was at this point that the step-by-step strategy started to come unstuck. When Cornwallis set out in January 1781 he found himself marching in a frustrating circle, usually failing to catch the Patriot forces, unable to destroy them when he did, and discovering very

little in the way of Loyalist support. By April he had had enough. What had worked in Georgia and South Carolina clearly was not going to work here. There was nothing for it but to pull back and go over to the defensive.

At least that is how he should have reacted if he had followed Clinton's instructions. But Cornwallis was a fighting general, cast in the same optimistic mould as Burgoyne. What he decided to do instead was continue his march north and take the war into Virginia. There was already a small British force there, under Benedict Arnold of turncoat fame, operating out of Portsmouth with the support of the Royal Navy. If Cornwallis were to bring his men up alongside Arnold's the two of them could really teach the Virginians a lesson.

Cornwallis crossed the Virginian border in May. The French and Americans, who already had a tentative scheme afoot to trap Arnold, found a bigger prize coming their way. Till now they had never managed to get their act together, but gradually the factors that had frustrated their efforts had been identified and corrected. Washington needed reinforcements? The French put General Rochambeau and 8,000 men ashore at Newport. The Allies needed command of the sea? The French promised to commit their main battlefleet, twenty-seven ships of the line under de Grasse. Most important of all, the French were able to insist that Chesapeake Bay be the focal point of the next campaign. Though Washington was reluctant – he wanted to make an all out effort against New York – he was won round in the end, Chesapeake Bay it would be.

Cornwallis had a good summer in Virginia. He chased Governor Jefferson from Richmond and the Virginia legislature from Charlottesville, burned a heap of stores and then moved to the coast to take ship for New York. To his surprise he found new orders from Clinton, telling him to stay where he was and set up a permanent base at Yorktown on the James Peninsula. Confident that the Royal Navy would keep him supplied, Cornwallis agreed to do so.

During August the players began moving into

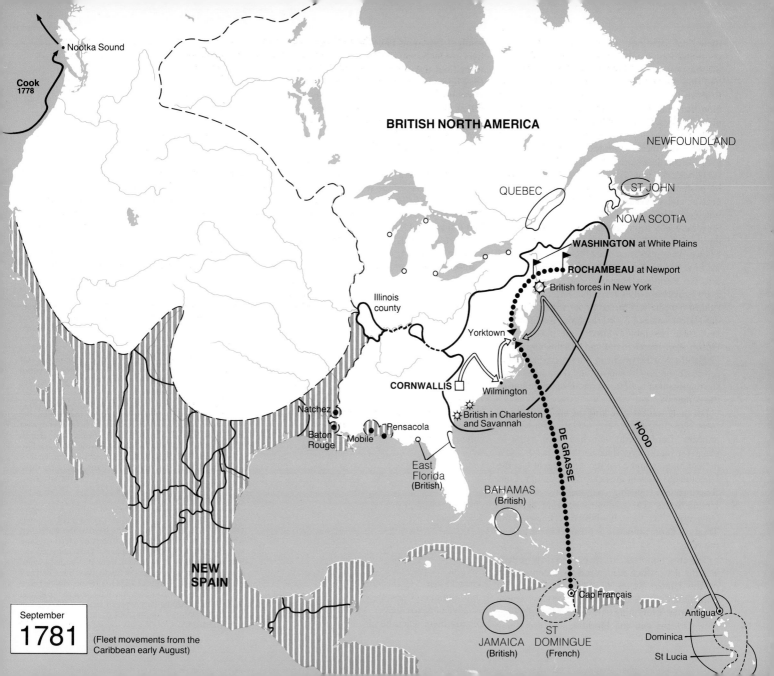

Cook
1778

• Nootka Sound

BRITISH NORTH AMERICA

NEWFOUNDLAND

QUEBEC

ST JOHN

NOVA SCOTIA

WASHINGTON at White Plains

ROCHAMBEAU at Newport

☼ British forces in New York

Illinois
county

Yorktown

CORNWALLIS ☐

Wilmington

☼ British in Charleston
and Savannah

Natchez

Baton
Rouge

Mobile

Pensacola

East
Florida
(British)

BAHAMAS
(British)

DE GRASSE

HOOD

**NEW
SPAIN**

Cap Français

JAMAICA
(British)

ST
DOMINGUE
(French)

Antigua

Dominica

St Lucia

September
1781

(Fleet movements from the
Caribbean early August)

their final positions. Cornwallis completed his concentration at Yorktown. Rochambeau and Washington set out from New York via New Jersey and the Delaware. De Grasse departed Cap Français, St Domingue, and reappeared at the mouth of Chesapeake Bay. The surprise was complete. There was not a single British battleship in sight.

The only hope for Cornwallis now was that the main British fleet – on its way from the Caribbean via New York – would be able to beat de Grasse out of position. On 5 September British Admirals Graves and Hood did their best but, with only nineteen ships against de Grasse's twenty-four, they were not strong enough. They withdrew to await reinforcements, leaving Cornwallis to face a Franco-American army more than twice the size of his own. He held on till 17 October when, boxed into the Yorktown perimeter and taking increasingly heavy casualties from the batteries arrayed against him, he was forced to ask for terms. Two days later, watched by Washington, Rochambeau and their assembled forces, the 8,000-strong British army marched out and laid down its arms. England's North American enterprise had come full circle, finding its end within fifteen miles of its starting-point at Jamestown on the opposite side of the peninsula.

For there was no mistaking the finality of Yorktown. 'Oh God, it's all over,' said the British prime minister, Lord North, who had been trying to resign for years – ever since Saratoga, in fact. Now he had his way and even the intransigent George III could not prevent the new prime minister, Lord Rockingham, opening negotiations with the United States. The preliminaries were signed in November 1782, the definitive treaty, known as the Treaty of Paris, ratified in September of the following year.[1]

The most important article of the Treaty of Paris was the first, which recognized the independence of the United States of America. Subsequent paragraphs gave the new nation its simple boundaries: everything east of the Mississippi bar New Orleans and the Floridas, and everything south of the Great Lakes and the provincial frontiers of Quebec and Nova Scotia. The boundaries turned out to be less precise on the ground than they appeared to be on contemporary maps, in some places because the maps were wrong, in others because there were alternative versions of the provincial frontiers. The first fault made a nonsense of the north-west corner which was meant to be formed by a line running due west from the Lake of the Woods to the Mississippi. In reality, the source of the Mississippi lies to the south of the Lake of the Woods. The second led to a long standing dispute over the frontier between Maine (at this time still a district of Massachusetts) and Canada and, of more immediate importance, an altercation with Spain over the northern limits of west Florida. It was 1795 before the Spanish conceded the line required by the US government.[2]

In the Caribbean the British were able to insist on a restitution of the pre-war positions. This result, an unexpectedly satisfactory one from their point of view, they owed largely to a fine naval victory over the French at the Battle of Saintes in the Lesser Antilles in 1792. Admiral Rodney, whose faulty dispositions had been a significant factor in the Yorktown debacle, retrieved his reputation and Britain's fortunes by disrupting the French line of battle, forcing the French flagship to strike its colors and capturing Admiral de Grasse.

1 The British had already lost in two other areas. In 1778 George Clark led a force from Pittsburgh (the civilian development of Fort Pitt) down the Ohio to the Mississippi where he raised the American flag over the French-Canadian settlements on the left bank. The area was subsequently incorporated in the state of Virginia as Illinois county. And in 1779 the Spanish entered the war and proceeded to reduce the various posts that constituted western Florida (Natchez and Baton Rouge that year, Mobile in 1780 and Pensacola in 1781). At the peace treaty the disheartened British ceded them eastern Florida too. The Spanish also recovered control of Belize.

One positive achievement recorded by the British in these unhappy years was Captain Cook's exploration of the Pacific, the third phase of which brought him to Nootka Sound, Vancouver Island, for a month's refit (see the map on the previous page, dated 1781). The direct gain to geographical knowledge that resulted from this visit was small but the crew were able to collect a number of sea-otter pelts and the huge profit they made on these when they sold them at Canton on the homeward leg soon came to the ears of the English and American companies that traded in furs. As a result a regular traffic began which brought anything up to a dozen ships a year to this previously unvisited coast.

2 Until well into the 1790s the Spanish and British held on to various forts on the US side of the border, the Spanish because they viewed the northern frontier of west Florida differently from the Americans, the British because the Americans were not trying very hard to recompense the Loyalists for their losses, something they had promised to do in the Treaty of Paris. The last of these posts to be evacuated were the ones held by the Spaniards in the south. They agreed to go in 1795 but did not actually do so until 1798.

Worth noting is the extension of British sovereignty over the north-west of Canada, of which a small section is visible on the map. The area lay beyond the watershed which defined the Hudson's Bay Company's territory, and so was open to freelance trappers. They obtained the financial backing they needed from the business community in Montreal, where the North-West Fur Company was set up for the purpose in 1783. The date can be taken to mark the formal incorporation of the area in the British sphere. The dividing line between this and the Russian sector (present-day Alaska) was eventually fixed at the 141°W in 1825.

64

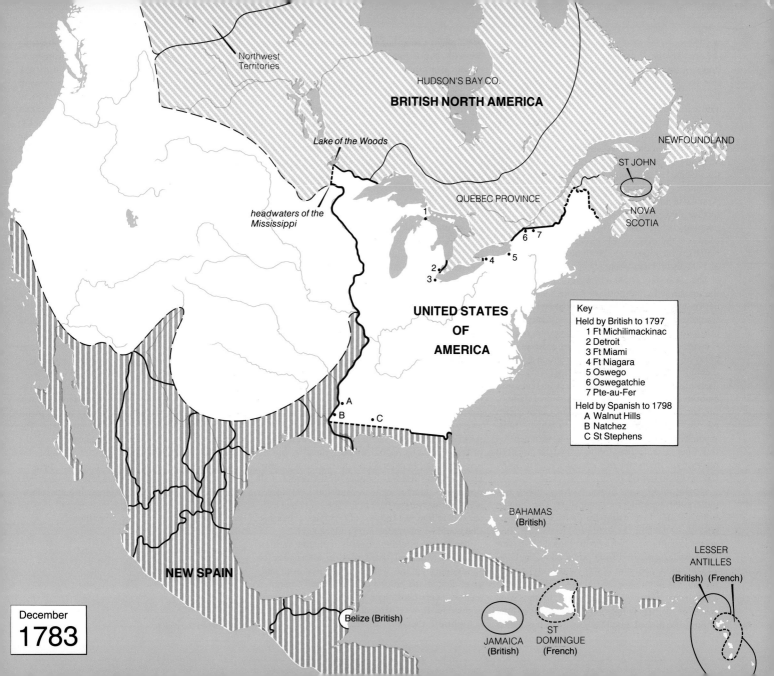

Northwest
Territories

HUDSON'S BAY CO.

BRITISH NORTH AMERICA

NEWFOUNDLAND

Lake of the Woods

ST JOHN

QUEBEC PROVINCE

NOVA
SCOTIA

*headwaters of the
Mississippi*

1

6 7

2
3

4
5

**UNITED STATES
OF
AMERICA**

Key
Held by British to 1797
  1 Ft Michilimackinac
  2 Detroit
  3 Ft Miami
  4 Ft Niagara
  5 Oswego
  6 Oswegatchie
  7 Pte-au-Fer
Held by Spanish to 1798
  A Walnut Hills
  B Natchez
  C St Stephens

A
B   C

BAHAMAS
(British)

NEW SPAIN

LESSER
ANTILLES
(British) (French)

Belize (British)

JAMAICA
(British)

ST
DOMINGUE
(French)

December
1783

If the Treaty of Paris determined the exterior limits of the American Republic, establishing its internal divisions required further political debate. Even within the settled area of the original Thirteen States there were boundary disputes, notably one between New York and New Hampshire which was resolved only by the elevation of the disputed zone into a fourteenth state, Vermont (1791). The major issue, however, was the disposal of the immense, largely unsettled and sometimes barely explored lands west of the Appalachians. Here the decision was to create further new states as and when the lands were peopled. In the case of Kentucky and Tennessee counties, the process was already well advanced, which enabled the two to be admitted to the Union in 1792 and 1796 respectively.

This procedure could not, as yet, be extended to the unpeopled areas north of Kentucky and south of Tennessee. Nevertheless, Congress set up a framework for the future development of the northern sector, appointing a governor for the 'Territory North-West of the Ohio River' and going on record as envisaging its eventual development into three to five separate states (1787). As to the southern zone, plans for it had to remain in embryo as long as Georgia maintained its claim to this territory. With the exception of Connecticut, all the other states had ceded their trans-Appalachian rights to the Federal government by this time. Connecticut relinquished its 'western reserve' on the south side of Lake Erie in 1800; Georgia held out till 1802.

During these years British North America was undergoing a parallel reorganization. The aim was to make suitable provision for the 80,000 Loyalists who chose to quit the United States rather than accept its authority. Nova Scotia took 20,000, New Brunswick (separated from Nova Scotia in 1794) 14,000, and Upper and Lower Canada (formed by the division of Quebec Province in 1791) 6,000 and 1,000 respectively. The rest went to the West Indies or the British Isles. The exodus was of little importance to the United States with its population of 5 million and an annual increase of 100,000. It was of major significance to British North America, boosting its population by 15 percent and changing its character from predominantly French Canadian to near enough half British.[1]

The territorial rearrangements made in the United States and Canada in the decade following the Treaty of Paris had considerable implications for the future. There is no denying, however, that the most important development of these years was the creation and smooth operation of the machinery of Federal government in the United States. In this process the leading role was played by George Washington, who presided over the Constitutional Congress which determined the form of the government, served two terms as President of the United States and, last but by no means least, refused to stand for a third. By the time he retired from public life in 1797 at the age of sixty-six, he had well earned Henry Lee's famous enconium: 'first in war, first in peace, first in the hearts of his countrymen.'[2]

As the American revolution passed into history its place at the center of the world stage was taken by the series of upheavals that constituted the French Revolution. At first the similarities between the two events seemed more important than the disparities but before many months had passed it was clear that a French revolutionary was a very different animal from his American counterpart. Washington was flattered to be sent the keys of the Bastille by his old friend Lafayette, but he was not going to extend his approval to a government in Paris that was lopping off the heads of all opponents, fancied or real. And the 1794 decree abolishing slavery in the French colonies must have seemed to him just the sort of precipitate measure that could be guaranteed to produce anarchy.

The French could reasonably reply that in their desperate situation there was no alternative to summoning up the whirlwind of total war and, given that all the powers of Europe had combined against them, it is difficult to deny the force of their argument. It was particularly applicable in the Caribbean theater where the revolutionary ideology was France's only means of offsetting England's naval superiority. And it did bring some remarkable successes. Though the English took most of the French islands in 1793–4, the news of the abolition of slavery enabled the French to launch an effective counter-offensive. In the end the British suppressed the black rebellions in the Lesser Antilles and established control over the entire chain, but on St Domingue the alliance between the French and the liberated blacks proved strong enough to checkmate the British. A particularly virulent outbreak of yellow fever completed the discomfiture of the British expeditionary force which was finally withdrawn in 1797.[3]

The sad story of Indian decline was punctuated in the late eighteenth century by the evolution of a new native culture, that of the Horse Indians of the Great Plains. The plains had always been inhabited, but the lot of the buffalo hunters before the introduction of the horse was, even by Indian standards, singularly harsh and unrewarding. The horse transformed the situation. Buffalo hunting became a symbol of the good life, the tepees of the nomad the hallmark of a proud and assured community. The cultural focus lay in the Black Hills of South Dakota and it was the Dakota Indians, more familiarly known as the Sioux, who were the strongest and most numerous of the Horse Indian tribes. However, the new prosperity of the plains attracted unrelated peoples from far afield. The Comanche, an offshoot of the Shoshone of the Great Basin, entered the area from the west; the Cheyenne and Cree, both Algonkian-speaking tribes, from the east and north. By the year 1800 there were probably 100,000 Horse Indians following the buffalo herds, whose numbers have been variously estimated at 25 to 50 million.[4]

1 For notes see p. 106.

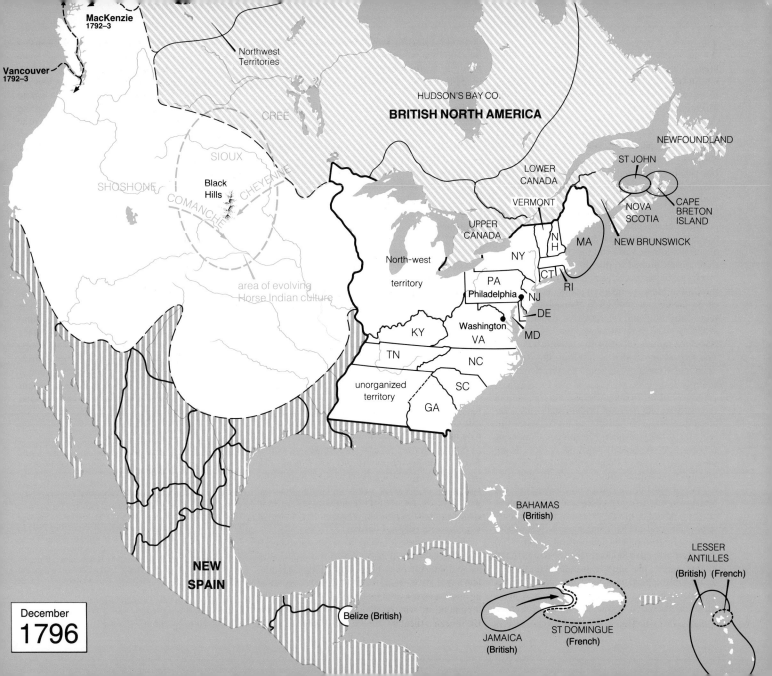

MacKenzie
1792–3

Vancouver
1792–3

Northwest
Territories

CREE

HUDSON'S BAY CO.

BRITISH NORTH AMERICA

NEWFOUNDLAND

SIOUX

SHOSHONE

Black
Hills

CHEYENNE

COMANCHE

area of evolving
Horse Indian culture

LOWER
CANADA

ST JOHN

NOVA
SCOTIA

CAPE
BRETON
ISLAND

VERMONT

UPPER
CANADA

NEW BRUNSWICK

NH

MA

North-west
territory

NY

CT

RI

PA

Philadelphia

NJ

DE

Washington

MD

KY

VA

TN

NC

unorganized
territory

SC

GA

BAHAMAS
(British)

**NEW
SPAIN**

LESSER
ANTILLES

(British) (French)

Belize (British)

JAMAICA
(British)

ST DOMINGUE
(French)

December
1796

In 1799 Napoleon Bonaparte seized power in France, inaugurating the spectacular adventure known as the French Empire. Essentially this was a European affair but, Napoleon's ambitions being as limitless as his energies, he found time to include America in his plans. His basic idea was to make France a New World power again by forcing Spain to return Louisiana. In 1800, after appropriate bullying, the Spanish signed the agreement Napoleon wanted, although the actual handover was to be delayed until such time as Napoleon could get a governor and a garrison into New Orleans.

Achieving this posed problems. In the first place Napoleon could not despatch any major expedition overseas while he was at war with Britain, for his ships were confined to port by the Royal Navy's blockade. In the second, any French operations in the Gulf of Mexico would require the use of a base on St Domingue and, given the political set-up there, no one could be sure that this would be available. The first problem was solved when Napoleon signed a truce with the British in 1802. The second he decided to tackle in the way that came most naturally to him, by direct military action.

Control of St Domingue had been lost not, as originally feared, to Great Britain but to one of the black generals who had played a leading part in repelling the British invasion, Toussaint L'Ouverture. Nominally loyal to France, Toussaint made no use of French officialdom and governed as he saw fit. No doubt Napoleon could have bargained with him, but he decided instead to bring him down. To this end he prepared an expeditionary force of 20,000 men, entrusted it to his brother-in-law, General Leclerc, and made it clear to him that he expected speedy and ruthless action.

Leclerc arrived in St Domingue in early 1802 and by the summer had the situation there pretty well under control. Toussaint was arrested and sent off to exile in France, where he died the next year. Most of the country was occupied by French troops. But there were already signs that Napoleon's plan for reviving a French dominion in the Americas was not going to have an easy conclusion. The United States government had got wind of what was going on and was making its displeasure plain.

The Americans were not concerned about Toussaint or his black followers. Indeed, the slave owners of the south were more than happy to see him and his lieutenants disposed of. But no American wanted to see Louisiana pass from a weak power like Spain to a strong one like France. The presumption had been that Louisiana would become US territory one day and do so without too much fuss. The possibility that French troops might appear along the Mississippi put this comfortable scenario in jeopardy, and when the news of the retrocession was confirmed the cry went up for war.

President Jefferson stayed calm. He made contact with the British just in case it did come to war and found that the British were eager for an alliance. But he put his main trust in an offer to buy New Orleans. He instructed his representative in Paris to offer up to $7.5 million. At first Bonaparte was not having it. Then he got news from St Domingue which made him think again. Of the 35,000 men he had sent to the island in the course of the year, two-thirds, including General Leclerc, had succumbed to yellow fever. To sustain French rule there he would have to send as many again, with no guarantee that they would fare any better or live any longer. Worse still, it was clear that France's window of opportunity was closing. The British were preparing to challenge Napoleon's European order once again and soon the seas would cease to be safe for French shipping. In these circumstances it was unlikely he could hold on to St Domingue, let alone Louisiana.

His mind made up, Napoleon acted quickly. It was not a question of $7.5 million for New Orleans, he told the American negotiators, but of $15 million for Louisiana. And on near enough these terms the transaction – often referred to as the biggest real-estate deal in history – was signed and sealed within the month. The United States had almost doubled its area and paid no more than 4 cents an acre to do so.

The territory gained by the Louisiana Purchase was only half the good news. Almost as important was the fact that the USA now had indefinite boundaries in the west. By deliberately blurring the definition of Louisiana, Jefferson was able to start talking about American claims to Texas, western Florida and the whole Pacific seaboard north of the California settlements. The Spanish were struck dumb at the suggestion that Texas and west Florida could even be considered as subjects for discussion and for the moment Jefferson did not press these issues. What he did do was gain firm title to the lands of the north-west by despatching Captains Lewis and Clark of the US Army overland to the Pacific. Their thirty-one-man expedition, preparations for which had been started before Napoleon had agreed to part with Louisiana, set out from St Louis in 1804, wintered among the Mandan, a Siouan tribe still faithful to the sedentary life, crossed the Rockies in the summer of 1805 to reach the Columbia river in October and its estuary a month later. The political importance of this exploratory journey hardly needs stressing. The expedition is also remarkable for the fact that it lost only one man during the twenty-eight months it took to get to the Pacific and back – and he died of appendicitis.[1]

1 Also visible in this map are some important changes in the political structure of the USA, notably the admission of Ohio as a state (1803), the subsequent division of the remaining area north-west of the Ohio between the Indiana and Michigan territories (1805), and the creation of two administrative districts within the Louisiana Purchase, the District of Louisiana and the Orleans territory (1804–5). In Canada the island of St John was renamed Prince Edward Island (hereafter abbreviated to PEI) in 1798 in honor of a member of the British royal family who was military governor of Halifax at the time, but who is perhaps better remembered – if he is remembered at all – as the father of Queen Victoria. In the Caribbean note the departure of the French from the western half of St Domingue (they clung on for a while in the east). This left Toussaint's successor Dessalines in charge. In 1804 he started calling himself Emperor of Haiti, this being the original Arawak name of the island.

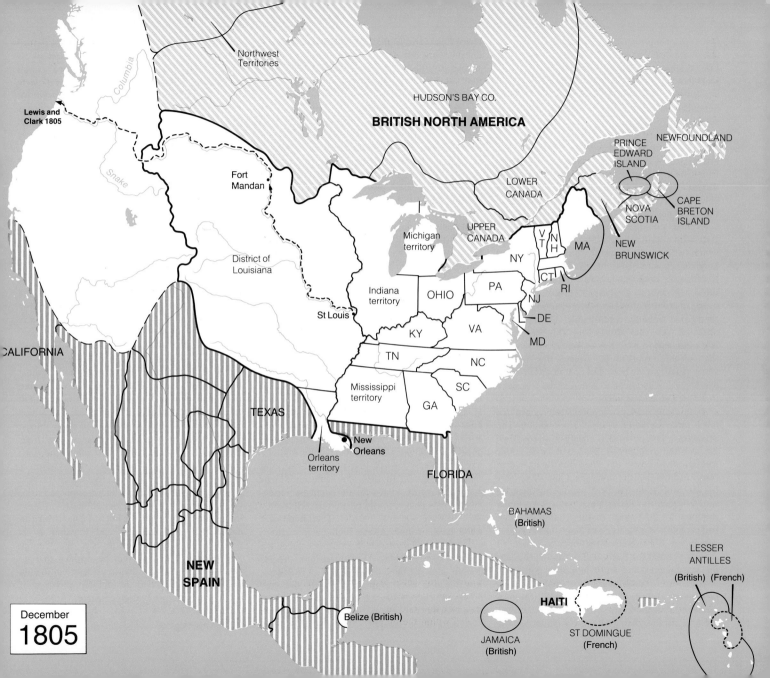

Northwest
Territories

Columbia

Lewis and
Clark 1805

Snake

HUDSON'S BAY CO.

BRITISH NORTH AMERICA

NEWFOUNDLAND

PRINCE
EDWARD
ISLAND

CAPE
BRETON
ISLAND

LOWER
CANADA

NOVA
SCOTIA

NEW
BRUNSWICK

Fort
Mandan

District of
Louisiana

Michigan
territory

UPPER
CANADA

V
T

N
H

MA

NY

Indiana
territory

OHIO

PA

CT

RI

St Louis

NJ

DE

KY

VA

MD

CALIFORNIA

TN

NC

Mississippi
territory

SC

TEXAS

GA

Orleans
territory

New
Orleans

FLORIDA

BAHAMAS
(British)

LESSER
ANTILLES

**NEW
SPAIN**

(British) (French)

Belize (British)

JAMAICA
(British)

HAITI

ST DOMINGUE
(French)

December
1805

For the first twenty years of its existence the United States had remained content with its original boundaries. The Louisiana Purchase produced a radical change in attitudes. Successive administrations maintained, and some of them seem to have half believed, that the deal struck with France had given America a claim to both Texas and the Floridas. More cogently, they argued that these provinces were bound to pass from Spain to the United States in the not too distant future. Population pressure made it inevitable. The Spanish would do well to sell out before they were pushed out.

At first the Spanish refused to talk. These American territorial pretensions seemed to them so self-evidently absurd that to discuss them would be giving them a dignity that they did not merit. But the issue would not go away. In 1810 American settlers in the part of west Florida closest to Louisiana took matters into their own hands. They repudiated Spanish control and asked for and obtained American jurisdiction. This was gradually extended over the rest of west Florida during the next three years on the grounds that the province had originally been part of Louisiana (which was true) and had been included in the Louisiana Purchase (which was not).

By this time the United States was engaged in a much more ambitious attempt at expansion. The objective was to conquer Canada and so complete the task the founders of the American Republic had set themselves, the liberation of all North America from British colonial rule. The pretext for the war, which began in 1812, was the high-handed way in which the Royal Navy treated American shipping, for the British, on the grounds that they had established a blockade of Napoleon's empire, demanded and exercised the right to search all shipping bound for Europe. To many Americans this was unacceptable and a modest majority was obtained for a declaration of war that would, its proponents declared, bring glorious victory in a matter of months.

Despite some stirring actions on and around the Great Lakes and on the high seas, the War of 1812 did not work out well for the United States. The British gave about as good as they got in fighting that never achieved more than local significance, while New England, which had been against the war from the start, suffered severely from British blockade. By Christmas 1814 both sides agreed to cease hostilities and reinstate the pre-war frontiers. The only useful victories the warhawks could claim were over the Indian allies of the British. Tecumseh, a Shawnee who had put together a confederacy rather like Pontiac's (though this time with the Americans not the British as the enemy) was disposed of in one of the battles in the vicinity of Detroit, while the Creeks, the most powerful Indian tribe in the Mississippi territory, were given a drubbing by Andrew Jackson of Tennessee in 1813–14. For the Indians these were more than set-backs; they put in jeopardy all the remaining lands they held east of the Mississippi.

Andrew Jackson was the most significant figure to emerge in this rather disappointing decade. 'Tough as old hickory', was the admiring verdict of the troops he led, and in both his military and political careers he displayed a frontier directness that contrasted sharply with the careful manners of the easterners who had so far had a near monopoly of high federal office. As a soldier, Jackson's finest hour was the clobbering he gave a British force attempting to seize New Orleans in the closing phase of the War of 1812. Diplomatically, it was his forays into east Florida that produced the most significant results. In 1814 and again in 1817 he occupied Pensacola and dealt out summary punishment to anyone he considered guilty of offences on the American side of the border. Their impotence when faced with Jackson's high-handed actions was one of the factors which finally persuaded the Spanish to sell Florida to the United States. The $5 million deal, dignified as the Treaty of Idelfonso, was signed in 1819. Appropriately, the first governor of the new 'Florida territory' was none other than Old Hickory himself.[1]

As part of the Treaty of Idelfonso the Spanish obtained an admission that Texas was not part of the Louisiana Purchase and a definition of its frontiers that made this plain. The price was an agreement to limit Spain's claims in the north west to the area below latitude 42°N. A year earlier (in 1818) the British had accepted the 49th parallel as the boundary between Canada and the US from the Lake of the Woods to the Rockies, so the only part of North America with a question mark still hanging over it was the 'Oregon Country', the land west of the Rockies and north of the Spanish claim. The Americans offered to settle this issue by simply extending the existing frontier to the Pacific, but the British turned down the US proposal. They were right to do so, at least in the short run. The New York-based America Fur Company signally failed to make a go of its outpost on the Columbia (Astoria, founded in 1811), whereas its Montreal-based rival, the North-West Fur Company, acted with vigor, establishing a string of posts on the Fraser and Columbia. By 1821 these were turning in such a handsome profit that the Hudson's Bay Company was pleased to add them to its network.[2]

Shortly after sorting out its frontier problems with the United States, the Spanish Empire expired. Napoleon had thrown the colonial bureaucracy into confusion by deposing the Spanish Bourbons in 1808 and, though his downfall was followed by the return of the dynasty, it proved impossible to restore the old way of doing things. One by one the American provinces declared their independence, the southernmost taking the lead. Mexico, though rocked by revolts, stayed officially loyal until 1821 when Colonel Agustin de Iturbide joined one of the rebellions he was supposed to be suppressing. After making himself master of Mexico City, he announced the birth of a new Mexican nation with independence and freedom as its watchwords. Alas, Iturbide was no George Washington. The next year he decided that he deserved a better title than president and in July 1822 Mexico City had the dubious privilege of watching him crown himself emperor.[1]

1 For notes see p. 106.

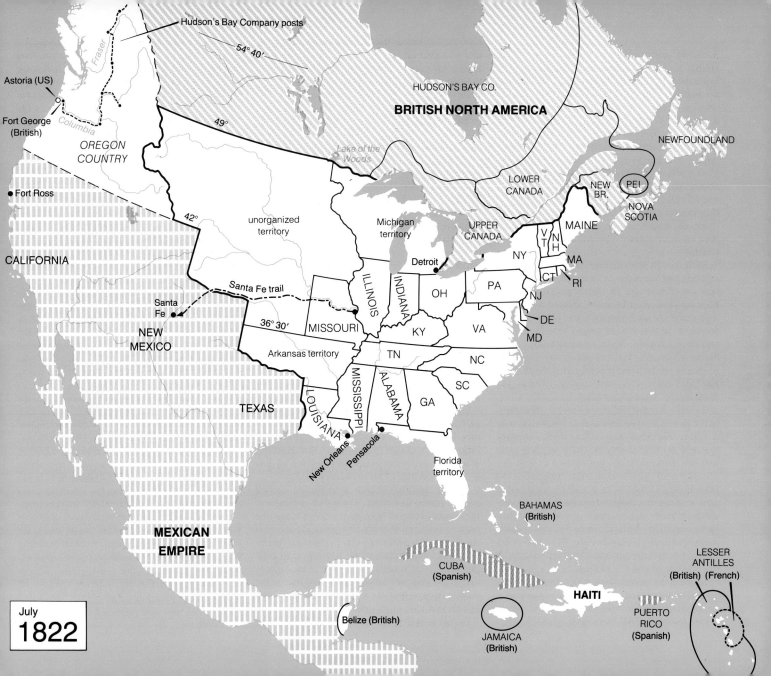

Hudson's Bay Company posts

54° 40'

Fraser

HUDSON'S BAY CO.

BRITISH NORTH AMERICA

NEWFOUNDLAND

Astoria (US)

Columbia

49°

Fort George
(British)

*OREGON
COUNTRY*

Lake of the
Woods

LOWER
CANADA

NEW
BR.

PEI

NOVA
SCOTIA

Fort Ross

42°

unorganized
territory

Michigan
territory

UPPER
CANADA

MAINE

VT

NH

NY

MA

CALIFORNIA

Detroit

ILLINOIS

INDIANA

OH

PA

CT

RI

NJ

Santa Fe trail

Santa
Fe

NEW
MEXICO

36° 30'

MISSOURI

KY

VA

DE

MD

Arkansas territory

TN

NC

TEXAS

MISSISSIPPI

ALABAMA

SC

GA

LOUISIANA

New Orleans

Pensacola

Florida
territory

**MEXICAN
EMPIRE**

BAHAMAS
(British)

LESSER
ANTILLES
(British) (French)

CUBA
(Spanish)

HAITI

PUERTO
RICO
(Spanish)

July
1822

Belize (British)

JAMAICA
(British)

Iturbide's Mexican Empire proved short-lived. In less than a year a revolt led by another soldier, Santa Anna, had forced him into exile and restored a republican form of government. This time the idea was to take the United States as a model, but the federal and democratic constitution that was hailed as the start of a new era lasted no longer than its predecessors. There was simply no tradition of self-government on which to build: power was something that had always been imposed from above. Within a few years the power was being wielded by Santa Anna who, though content to call himself president, added so many honorifics ('his most serene highness', 'the supreme power') that his government was indistinguishable from Iturbide's.

Brief though its existence was, the federal constitution had one major achievement to its credit, a new set of rules for the development of Texas. Mexicans had never been attracted to this remote area and could not be persuaded to settle there. In consequence it remained grossly underpopulated and there was a real risk of it passing to the United States by default. What about letting American settlers in on condition that they toed the Mexican line? Was not that less dangerous than leaving the place empty? The policy was agreed and the Americans invited in. By 1835 there were 20,000 of them in the province, as against a mere 5,000 Mexicans.

Figures like these suggest that trouble was on the way whoever was in charge, but if anything extra was needed Santa Anna was pleased to supply it. His style of government was autocratic and centralizing. He had no time at all for the constitution that theoretically safeguarded the Texans' local liberties and he made this plain to their delegates. The Texans' response was equally uncompromising. They declared their independence from Mexico and occupied the two frontier posts of the Alamo and Goliad.

Santa Anna took the field with an army of 6,000 men. He threatened all rebels with instant execution and, if this made little difference at the Alamo, where few of the 180 defenders survived the Mex-ican army's furious assault, it led to a grim scene at Goliad a few weeks later. The 350 American volunteers garrisoning Goliad had surrendered on a promise of fair treatment. On Santa Anna's direct orders they were shot down in cold blood. For many American settlers this was enough; they headed east for the US border as fast as they could. Less than a thousand men stayed with Sam Houston, the last hope of the rebel cause.

Assuming that the campaign was now just a matter of pursuit, Santa Anna divided his forces. This enabled him to move fast, but it also meant that by the time he reached Houston's camp near the San Jacinto river he had barely 1,200 men with him, only a few hundred more than his opponent. He then compounded his folly by failing to set a proper guard. Sam Houston was not the man to miss a chance like this. Leading the Texans forward in line of battle, he reached the dozing Mexicans before they realized they were under attack. Half of them were slaughtered on the spot: the rest, including Santa Anna, were made prisoners. It was the victory Texas needed.

The Texans had rebelled on the assumption that if they won their war the United States would bring them into the Union. It turned out to be not quite as simple as that. The admission of Texas, which was a slave state, would upset the delicate political balance between slave and free. The anti-slavery party in Congress felt so strongly about this that they blocked Texas's application. All President Jackson could do for his old friend Sam Houston was recognize Texan independence. This he duly did on the last day of his presidency.

Slavery had now become a major and divisive issue in American politics. The founding fathers of the republic seem to have assumed that it was one of those problems that would go away as the nation developed. By and large slave labor was inefficient; the tobacco plantations, which were its original focus, were usually on the edge of bankruptcy and in the end free labor must surely render the slave economy obsolete. Unfortunately what happened was the exact opposite. The Industrial Revolution in England created an ever-escalating demand for cotton. The southern planters, helped by Eli Whitney's invention of the cotton gin, soon learned how to satisfy this and became rich doing so. In the south – roughly defined as the area below the Mason–Dixon line (the Maryland–Pennsylvania border) and the Ohio river – the number of slaves rose from 700,000 in 1790 to 2.5 million in 1840. And as slavery became more profitable so the southerners' defense of it became more vociferous. Whereas in 1787 the south's representatives had been prepared to see the north-west territory declared free, in 1820 they fought every inch of the way over the Louisiana Purchase. They wanted slavery recognized throughout the area. In the end they had to settle for the area south of 36° 30′ (the northern border of the Arkansas territory as shown on the map for 1822) plus Missouri. It was this uneasy bargain – the Missouri Compromise of 1820 – that the admission of Texas theatened.[1]

If Andrew Jackson had no solution to the problem of black slavery he had a decisive answer to the Indian question. As he saw it, trouble was inevitable so long as American settlers and Indian tribes tried to live cheek by jowl. He decided to move all the Indians currently living east of the Mississippi across the river and resettle them in the empty lands of the west.

What was involved is best visualized in the southern sector where the surviving Indians consisted of a few relatively large and easily identified tribal groups: the Cherokee, Creek, Chickasaw, Choctaw and Seminole. Between 1830 and 1835 all these peoples were forcibly transferred to reserves within what is now the state of Oklahoma. It was done, Jackson said, because the alternative was extinction, and most of the 60,000 Indians transferred did survive. On the other hand, it cannot have seemed such a good idea to the Indians at the time, for they lost their homes, much of their lifestyle and anything up to a quarter of their number.

1 The admission of Missouri was balanced by the separation of Maine from Massachusetts. In the next decade the balance was preserved with the admission of Arkansas as a slave state (1836) and Michigan as a free one (1837).

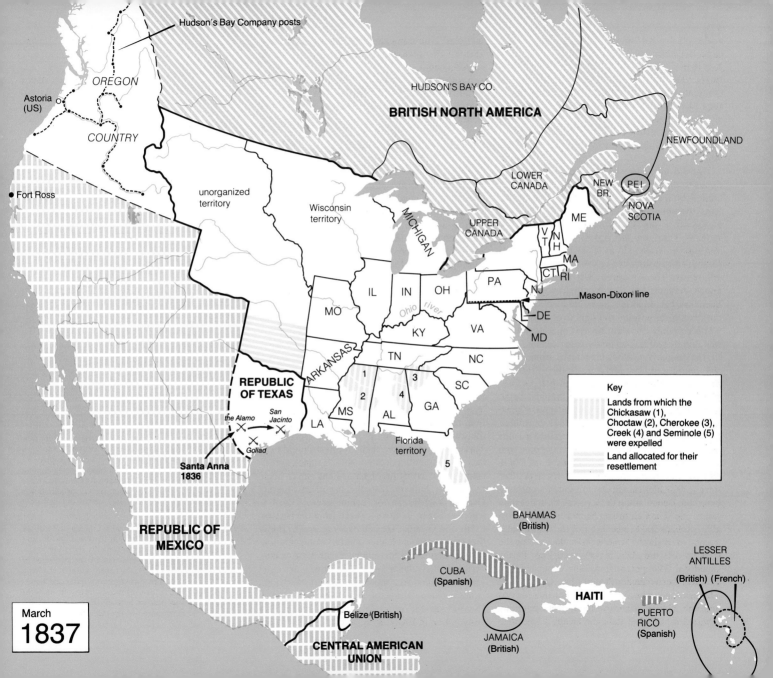

Hudson's Bay Company posts

OREGON

Astoria (US)

COUNTRY

● Fort Ross

HUDSON'S BAY CO.

BRITISH NORTH AMERICA

NEWFOUNDLAND

unorganized territory

Wisconsin territory

MICHIGAN

LOWER CANADA

PEI

NOVA SCOTIA

NEW BR.

ME

UPPER CANADA

VT
NH
MA
CT
RI

MO

IL

IN

OH

PA

NJ

DE

Mason-Dixon line

MD

Ohio river

KY

VA

ARKANSAS

TN

NC

REPUBLIC OF TEXAS

1

2

3

4

SC

GA

the Alamo

San Jacinto

MS

AL

Goliad

LA

Santa Anna 1836

Florida territory

5

Key

Lands from which the Chickasaw (1), Choctaw (2), Cherokee (3), Creek (4) and Seminole (5) were expelled

Land allocated for their resettlement

REPUBLIC OF MEXICO

BAHAMAS (British)

CUBA (Spanish)

LESSER ANTILLES

(British) (French)

HAITI

PUERTO RICO (Spanish)

Belize (British)

JAMAICA (British)

March **1837**

CENTRAL AMERICAN UNION

Deeply divided though they were on the slavery issue, the American people thought it the height of folly to let Texas slip from their grasp because of it. In the 1844 presidential election they chose the candidate who had made this his position from the start, James Polk of Tennessee. The electoral message was so clear that the annexation of Texas was arranged forthwith and the 'Lone Star State' was already in the Union by the time Polk took office.

This did not leave the new president short of things to do. His intention was to obtain for the United States the entire north-west (up to the Russian frontier at 54° 40′), the Mexican provinces of New Mexico and California and a frontier for the state of Texas on the Rio Grande. It was an immense program and, as far as Mexico was concerned, an unjustifiably aggressive one. Polk saw it differently. The Americans were already on the march and there was no stopping them now. If the Mexicans wanted to sell, he would buy: if they did not, then history would roll right over them.

It is certainly true that the next migratory wave was already building up in the American midwest. In 1841 a party of sixty-nine men, women and children set out from Missouri for the west coast, half of them going to Oregon and half to California. The next year more than a hundred took the trail to Oregon and the year after that it was 900. So began the wagon-train era. The 1843 expedition had 120 of the canvas-covered Conestoga wagons and took 5,000 head of cattle with them: the settlers were staking out their claims in the Willamette valley by the spring of 1844. By 1846 there were 4,000 Americans in Oregon and they outnumbered the Canadians in the territory by better than five to one. The Californian figures were less favorable, perhaps 700 as against 5,000 Mexicans, but if it came to a fight the Americans could count on the support of the US Navy's fledgling Pacific squadron. The potential of this command had already been demonstrated by Commodore Thomas Jones who, hearing a rumor that Mexico and the United States were at war, promptly stormed ashore and took the sleepy Californian capital of Monterey. However, he was four years too early, there was no war at all and he had to give it back again.[1]

Another war that never came off was the one with Britain over Oregon. It could have come to a fight if Polk had held to his original demand of a frontier at 54° 40′, for the British had a right to expect what they had already been offered several times, a frontier along the 49th parallel. They had previously turned this down, on the grounds that there was no American presence at all north of the Columbia. This was still true in 1846 but, with the demographic balance in the region as a whole rapidly swinging against them, the British wisely offered to settle for 49° if they could keep Vancouver Island in its entirety. Polk thought this was not good enough but the Senate, taking into consideration the fact that hostilities with Mexico were already under way, ratified the agreement.[2]

The Mexicans had proved intransigent. They had refused point-blank to discuss the sale of either New Mexico or California. They had hinted that they might be prepared to acquiesce, if the price was right, in the existing state of affairs as regards Texas, but they certainly would not allow that Texas ever had, or ever could have, its western frontier on the Rio Grande: the frontier was the River Nueces and there it must stay. In a purely legal sense it is difficult to fault the Mexican position, but in practical terms it was an invitation to disaster. President Polk simply accepted the Texans' view on where their frontiers should be – they had, after all, got Santa Anna's signed agreement to it even if this signature had never been ratified. In January 1846 the president ordered General Zachary Taylor, commander of the US forces in Texas, to move forward from the Nueces to the Rio Grande. He had every reason to think that this step would lead to military confrontation and strong grounds for believing that the outcome of this would be favorable to his cause.

1 The Californian offshoot of the Oregon trail terminated at Sutter's Fort, a trading-post and ranch run by a Swiss-German named John Sutter who occupied an important crossroads in early Californian history. Among his purchases was Fort Ross when the Russians no longer had any need for it (1841) and among his constructions was the mill in the Sacramento valley where the first gold turned up in 1848.

2 The other frontier dispute with Canada, concerning the sector betwen Maine on the one hand and Quebec and New Brunswick on the other, was finally settled in 1842.

Other points to notice on this map are the admission of Florida to the Union (1845), the organization of the Iowa territory, the union of the provinces of Upper and Lower Canada (1840) and, in the Caribbean, the expulsion of the Haitians from the eastern half of Hispaniola and the consequent reappearance of the Dominican Republic (1844).

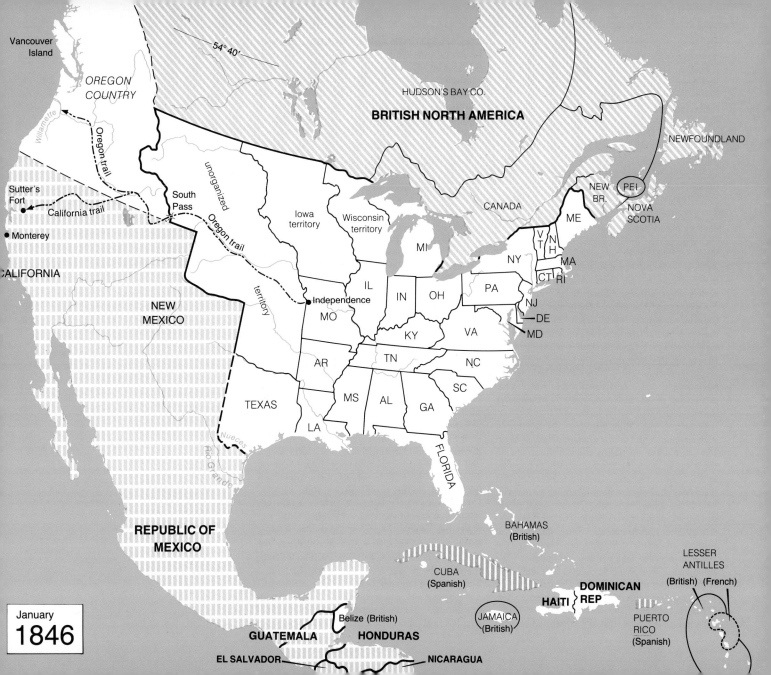

Vancouver
Island

54° 40'

HUDSON'S BAY CO.

BRITISH NORTH AMERICA

NEWFOUNDLAND

*OREGON
COUNTRY*

Willamette

Oregon trail

Sutter's
Fort

California trail

South
Pass

unorganized

Oregon trail

territory

Iowa
territory

Wisconsin
territory

CANADA

NEW
BR.

PEI

NOVA
SCOTIA

ME

MI

Monterey

CALIFORNIA

NEW
MEXICO

Independence

MO

IL

IN

OH

NY

VT
NH

MA

CT
RI

PA

NJ

DE

MD

KY

VA

AR

TN

NC

REPUBLIC OF
MEXICO

TEXAS

Nueces

Rio Grande

LA

MS

AL

GA

SC

FLORIDA

January
1846

BAHAMAS
(British)

CUBA
(Spanish)

DOMINICAN
REP

HAITI

JAMAICA
(British)

LESSER
ANTILLES

(British) (French)

PUERTO
RICO
(Spanish)

Belize (British)

GUATEMALA

HONDURAS

EL SALVADOR

NICARAGUA

In early 1846 President Polk was looking to the American Army to do three things: get the war with Mexico started, occupy all the territory to the north of the Gila River and the Rio Grande and inflict such a crushing defeat on Mexico's armed forces that its political leaders would be forced to sue for peace. The first two were easy. As expected, Mexican army units attacked General Zacharay Taylor's command as soon as he advanced to the Rio Grande and by May 1846 Mexico and America were formally at war. In June Colonel Kearny took the Santa Fe trail at the head of 1,600 troopers: by August he had achieved a near bloodless conquest of New Mexico. During the same period the combined efforts of the US Navy and a force of volunteers raised from the American element in the local population obtained the surrender of all the west coast settlements between Yerba Buena (shortly to be renamed San Francisco) and San Diego. There was a hiccup in California when the Mexican settlers rose against their new masters, reoccupied Los Angeles and cut up Kearny's escort as he rode in from New Mexico to take up his appointment as governor of the new territory, but this rebellion soon fizzled out. By the beginning of 1847 the United States was in firm possession of all the areas which it would later annex.

President Polk's third objective, the creation of such a commanding military position that the Mexicans would lose the ability and the will to sustain the struggle, took a little longer. By September 1847 Taylor had advanced to Monterrey and taken the town, but Polk felt he was moving too slowly, issuing too many communiqués and, worst of all, getting too popular back home. He decided – and though the judgement may have had political roots, it also made strategic sense – to put a new army in the field under a new commander. The commander was Winfield Scott, the army was 10,000 strong, and the US Navy put it ashore at Vera Cruz, within striking distance of Mexico City, in March 1847.

General Scott took the same road that Hernan Cortes had 300 years earlier. By early August 1847 he was looking down on Mexico City and towards the end of that month he won the battle of Churubusco over its defenders. This gave him the chance to advance on the capital but instead he offered an armistice to the Mexicans to give them time to mull over the American peace terms. However, the Mexicans still refused to accept the loss of the whole tier of provinces in the north: Texas maybe, but New Mexico and California?. . . not a chance! Anyway, they now had the great military leader Santa Anna as their president once more. His Texan misadventures forgiven, he had returned from exile in Havana in late 1846 and immediately begun bustling around trying to put heart into Mexico's disrupted forces. By February 1847 he was claiming to have fought General Taylor to a halt in a drawn battle at Buena Vista, south-west of Monterrey. In fact Buena Vista had been another defeat but the people of Mexico City were not to know that and they remained confident that their hero was the man to drive General Scott back from the gates of the capital. And Santa Anna did give the Americans their bloodiest battle yet, though he could neither win the day nor prevent their further advance. From the battlefield of Molina del Rey the Americans swept forward, taking Chapultepec Hill despite the legendary resistance of the boy cadets of Mexico's military academy, and setting up their guns on the rooftops of the surrounding monasteries. Faced with the threat of bombardment Mexico City surrendered and General Scott was able to lead his 'Army of Occupation' through the streets of the capital and into the *Zocalo*, the great square at its heart.

Five months later, in March 1848, the Mexican authorities signed the treaty President Polk had been determined to have all along. The United States got California, New Mexico and Texas, the latter with the Rio Grande frontier demanded from the start. There was a sweetener, for the United States made a payment of $15 million to the Mexican government, which was as much as it had paid out for the roughly comparable Louisiana Purchase of 1803. However, as the Mexicans were well aware, they could have got three times as much if they had chosen to sell their rights, rather than fight for them.

Most Americans were highly pleased with the treaty of Guadalupe Hidalgo which confirmed the United States' acquisition of these vast territories. Notable exceptions were Brigham Young and his followers of the Mormon faith. Some 5,000 members of this unorthodox fundamentalist sect had taken the Oregon trail to escape the persecutions inflicted on them by their fellow Americans. In the harsh landscape of Utah Brigham Young discovered the Mormons' promised land and under his leadership the first settlements were laid out within sight of the Great Salt Lake. Now the Mormons had to come to terms with the fact that the frontiers of the United States had advanced further and faster than they had and that they were not after all going to be able to create their own independent state of 'Deseret'.

Note the admission of Iowa to the Union (1846) and the way the residue of the Iowa territory has been returned to the unorganized category.

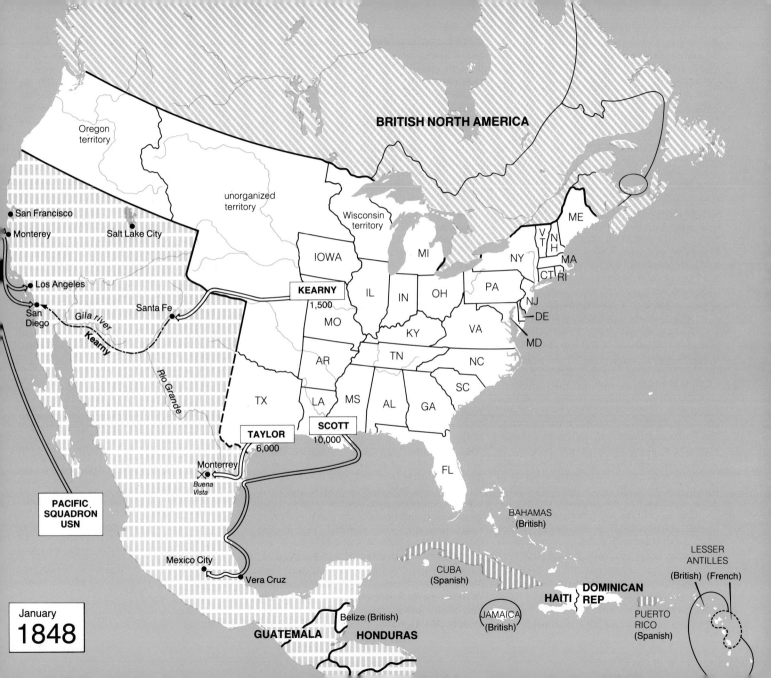

BRITISH NORTH AMERICA

Oregon
territory

unorganized
territory

Wisconsin
territory

● San Francisco
● Monterey

Salt Lake City

● Los Angeles

San
Diego

Gila river

Kearny

Santa Fe

Rio Grande

IOWA

MI

KEARNY
1,500

IL

MO

IN

OH

KY

AR

TN

NY

PA

VA

NC

ME

VT
NH
MA
CT RI

NJ
DE
MD

TX

LA

MS

SC

AL

GA

TAYLOR
6,000

SCOTT
10,000

FL

Monterrey
×
*Buena
Vista*

**PACIFIC
SQUADRON
USN**

Mexico City

Vera Cruz

BAHAMAS
(British)

CUBA
(Spanish)

JAMAICA
(British)

HAITI

DOMINICAN
REP

LESSER
ANTILLES
(British) (French)

PUERTO
RICO
(Spanish)

Belize (British)

GUATEMALA   **HONDURAS**

January
1848

If there were any Americans who felt that $15 million was too much to pay for New Mexico and California, their misgivings were soon put to rest. Even as the Treaty of Guadalupe Hidalgo was being signed there was a rumor going round San Francisco that gold had been found in the Sacramento valley. By the spring of 1848 the secret was out – the rivers on the Sierra Nevada side were awash with gold. San Francisco emptied as every able-bodied male headed for the valley, and the wider the news spread the hotter burned the gold fever. Would-be settlers who had just arrived in Oregon packed up again and headed south; Mexicans who were on their way out of California turned round and made their way back to the headwaters of the San Joaquin. At the year's end gold to the value of $3.7 million had been banked in San Francisco and, as many of the most promising sites remained unexplored, there was every reason to believe that the real bonanza was still to come.

In 1849 it was the east's turn to catch the bug. Gold fever seized hard-bitten farming folk in the hills and eager young clerks in New York offices. Everyone wanted to get rich quick, California was the place to do it and the only problem was how to get there before the gold ran out. Sixteen thousand easterners made the long haul round Cape Horn by sailing ship, 6,000 took the theoretically quicker passage to Panama by steamship and then on to San Francisco by whatever boats were available. From the midwest the route was overland, in wagon trains using the Oregon trail and its north California branch, or, in the case of an adventurous minority, a seemingly more direct route from Arkansas across the Texas panhandle to New Mexico, then via the Gila River valley to San Diego. Some 22,000 travelled the northern route, perhaps 3,000 the southern trail, making a grand total for the year, including Mexicans, of about 50,000.[1]

Surprisingly few people died during this migration despite outbreaks of cholera at several of the collecting points. Even fewer were to strike it rich when they got to California. Panning for gold was backbreaking work, deposits that could make a man's fortune were always exceptional, and most new arrivals abandoned their claims after a few unhappy months in the mining camps. But the 'forty-niners' and the equally large number of migrants who arrived the next year, boosted California's population well over the 100,000 mark (it had been only 14,000 when the first gold was found at Sutter's mill), and that was enough to get California's development off to a flying start. It was also enough to justify dispensing with the intermediate stage of territorial government and asking for immediate recognition as a state. California's admission to the Union, voted by Congress in August 1850 and signed into law by the president in September, was the real achievement of the gold-rush years.

California's constitution outlawed slavery, which meant that its application for statehood caused a great deal of heartache in the American south. Not only would its admission disturb the balance of fifteen slave states and fifteen free, but its geography violated the 36° 30′ line laid down in the Missouri Compromise of 1821. Admittedly the Missouri Compromise only referred to the Louisiana Purchase but the extension of the 36° 30′ line westward was the very least that the south expected when the territories acquired from Mexico came up for discussion. Many southerners wanted a line much further north, others argued for no restriction on slavery at all. Now California had jumped the gun in a totally unacceptable way. The southern states were outraged. South Carolina, always the most militant of them, even talked of seceding from the Union.

Politicians in both north and south found this willingness to threaten the Union so horrifying that they came together in an all-out effort to find a new compromise. Eventually, as part of a package deal that included the admission of California, it was agreed that slaves would be allowed into the territories of Utah (northern boundary 42°) and New Mexico. In theory this did not pre-empt the right of the people in these territories to vote themselves Free constitutions at a later stage. In practice it was a significant gain for the pro-slavery lobby, for once slavery was established it was notoriously difficult to eradicate. As a counterbalancing sop to the Abolitionists the traffic in slaves was prohibited in the nation's capital.[2]

The compromise of 1850 was greeted with signs of relief on all sides. Everyone felt that an issue that had been threatening to tear the republic apart had been fairly settled and that, with a bit of luck, the setlement would last for the foreseeable future. And, no doubt of it, the extremists on both sides did lose support in the period immediately following the compromise. There was much less talk of secession in the south, and in the north the Free Soil (Abolitionist) Party, which had polled a strong 10 percent in the 1848 presidential election, saw its share slump to 5 percent in 1852. The successful candidate on this occasion, Franklin Pierce of New Hampshire, was so moderate that he could be fairly described as inert. Apparently that was what the country wanted. He put the slave issue to sleep along with his audiences. The final tally showed that he had done equally well in both north (where he won every state except Massachusetts and Vermont) and south (all except Kentucky and Tennessee).

1 The scale of the movement along the Oregon trail led to friction with the Plains Indians, and the US Government decided something had to be done to police the route. Halfway along the trail there was a post that had been built by fur traders fifteen years earlier, Fort Laramie. The government bought it, garrisoned it and summoned the leaders of the Crow, Sioux, Cheyenne and Arapaho to a parley there in 1851. At the end of this the Indian chiefs put their marks on a treaty which defined their hunting grounds and excluded them from the line of the trail, while in return the government gave them annuities and other benefits.

2 A further tidying-up operation was the Federal Government's assumption of the Texan state debt. In return Texas agreed to give up its claim to the part of New Mexico east of the Rio Grande.

Other changes to be noted since the last map are the admission of Wisconsin as a state (1848) and the organization of the Oregon and Minnesota territories (1848 and 1849). In Canada the British created the colony of Vancouver Island in 1849 to compensate the Hudson's Bay Company for the loss of its posts in Oregon.

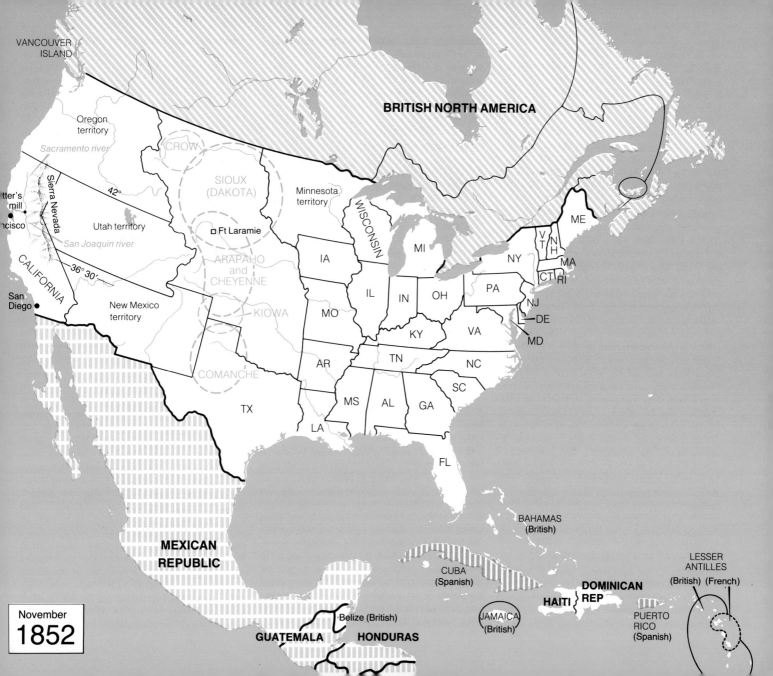

VANCOUVER
ISLAND

BRITISH NORTH AMERICA

Oregon
territory

Sacramento river

tter's
mill

ncisco

42°

Sierra Nevada

CROW

SIOUX
(DAKOTA)

Minnesota
territory

WISCONSIN

MI

ME

VT
NH

NY

MA

CALIFORNIA

San Joaquin river

36° 30'

Utah territory

■ Ft Laramie

ARAPAHO
and
CHEYENNE

IA

IL

IN

OH

PA

CT
RI

NJ

San
Diego

New Mexico
territory

KIOWA

MO

KY

VA

DE

MD

COMANCHE

AR

TN

NC

TX

MS

AL

GA

SC

LA

FL

MEXICAN
REPUBLIC

BAHAMAS
(British)

CUBA
(Spanish)

DOMINICAN
REP

HAITI

LESSER
ANTILLES
(British) (French)

JAMAICA
(British)

PUERTO
RICO
(Spanish)

Belize (British)

GUATEMALA

HONDURAS

November
1852

The compromise of 1850 quieted the slavery issue for less than four years: then the restless manoeuverings of the pro-slavery faction brought it to the center of the political arena again. This sounds wilful and, worse than that, foolish, for the slave states were palpably weaker in population and resources than the free, but the south's politicians were obsessed with the idea that slavery, if it were to survive at all, had to expand. The alternative notion – that the 'peculiar institution' would last longer the less attention it received – they refused to contemplate.

Some of the schemes floated in the south at this time were really wild. A campaign to reopen the African slave trade was a no-hoper if ever there was one and, given the known views of the northern states, it was equally impractical to talk of purchasing or, if Spain refused the proffered cash, annexing the island of Cuba. More realistic and therefore more threatening to the compromise of 1850 was the south's campaign to get slaves into the western territories. One aspect of this which was to have a permanent effect on the map of the United States was the proposal to build the first trans-continental railroad on a southern route. The intention was to ensure that the development of the west followed the slave-owning pattern: the difficulty was that the only practical line for a Southern Pacific railroad lay south of the Gila River, in Mexican territory. President Pierce, anxious to accommodate the southern lobby, sent Senator James Gadsden to Mexico City to see what could be done about this. The Senator persuaded Santa Anna – currently president for the fifth time – to sell (for $15 million, later reduced to $10 million) and the Gadsden purchase, as completed in 1854, brought the southern border of the United States to its present position.

The battle of the railroad routes now began in earnest. The slave states tried to get the administration's support for the Southern Pacific, the hard-line anti-slavery group countered with arguments for a Northern Pacific line, while Senator Stephen Douglas, the leading figure of the

Democratic Party, proposed a compromise based on the Central Pacific option. As part of his plan for doing so he lobbied hard and long for the introduction of territorial governments into the still-unorganized areas of the Louisiana Purchase which a Central Pacific railroad would have to cross. In 1854 he succeeded in getting the support of Congress for this. The Kansas–Nebraska Act of that year created the two territorial governments that he believed to be necessary not just for the development of the central zone and the furtherance of the railway project, but for the good health of the Union. It should have been a moment of triumph.

In fact it was a disaster. The passage of the Kansas–Nebraska act was followed by six years of increasing vituperation as the slavery issue broke surface again in its most intractable form. To obtain the south's support for his bill Douglas had agreed to allow slaves to be introduced into the Kansas and Nebraska territories. This flouted the Missouri Compromise of 1820, which expressly limited slavery within the Louisiana Purchase to the area below 36° 30′. Douglas tried to hide this concession under the liberal sounding rubric of 'Popular Sovereignty', the idea being that the settlers themselves would rule on the slavery question when the time came to draw up a state constitution. But this did not satisfy anyone. The north began to lose patience not just with the south but with the existing political parties.

In truth there could be no disguising the crucial appeasement in the Kansas–Nebraska act. It gave the south the opportunity of preserving its way of life forever. If the hope of the north was that the south would gradually evolve away from slavery, the fear of the south was that the north would one day be able to legislate slavery out of existence. For that it needed a two-thirds congressional majority, something that, given the existing pattern of development, could well come about before the end of the century. The only way the south could hope to stop it was by getting slaves into the territories and seeing that they stayed there.

All eyes now turned on Kansas, where the first

settlers were already arriving. Nearly all of them were northerners, their minds set against slavery, so if the southern lobby was going to get a slave constitution adopted it would have to move fast. The southerners rose to the occasion. Groups of 'border ruffians' – bushwackers from the neighboring slave state of Missouri – took over the polling stations. Corrupt officials counted or discarded ballots at will. The outcome was a triumph, a territorial legislature so vehement in its support of slavery that it refused to seat members with opposing views. A slave constitution seemed to be in the bag.

The settlers who were now pouring into Kansas were not prepared to countenance this. They called their own convention and drew up a free constitution. They armed themselves and matched raid with counter-raid. Kansas – 'Bleeding Kansas' as it became known to the orators of the time – became the setting for something ominously close to civil war.

The political crunch came in 1857. The leaders of the south demanded that President James Buchanan approve the slave constitution which, they claimed, the Kansans were calling for. They threatened the direst consequence if he did not. Buchanan, fearing for the Union, agreed to send the constitution to Congress with his blessing. The Senate passed it, but the House made its approval conditional on a favorable referendum. And that was really the end of the matter. When the good people of Kansas finally had their say they voted down the slave constitution by better than six to one. Kansas would enter the Union as a free state.[1]

The wounds sustained by 'Bleeding Kansas' went deep. Atrocities were perpetrated and reprisals exacted by both sides. The incident in which John Brown, a fanatic abolitionist, raided a supposedly pro-slavery settlement and murdered five of its inhabitants is a measure of the brutality and intransigence of the protagonists. Inevitably the nation was drawn down the same path. Violence even erupted on the floor of the Senate when Senator Charles Sumner of Massachusetts was beaten into unconsciousness by a southern

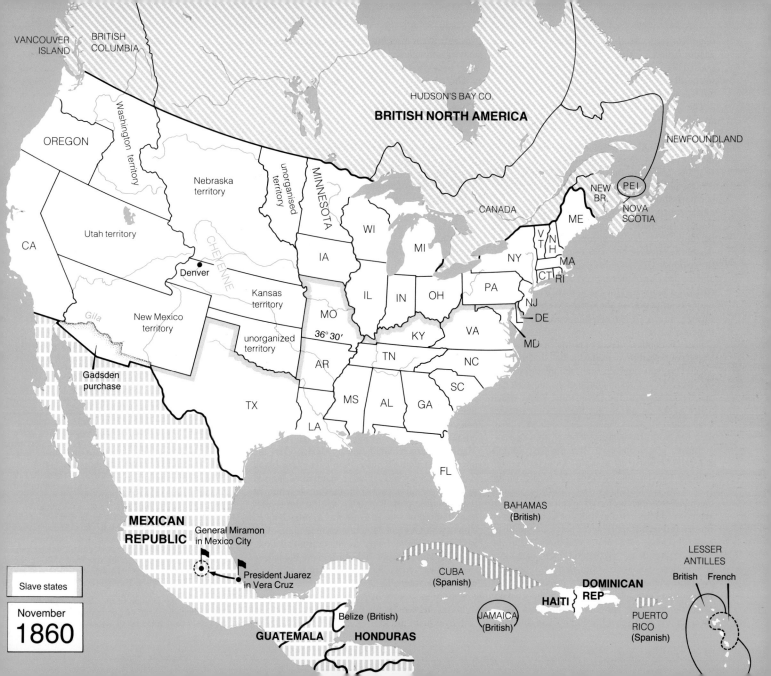

VANCOUVER ISLAND

BRITISH COLUMBIA

HUDSON'S BAY CO.

BRITISH NORTH AMERICA

NEWFOUNDLAND

OREGON

Washington territory

Nebraska territory

unorganised territory

MINNESOTA

CANADA

NEW BR.

PEI

NOVA SCOTIA

ME

Utah territory

CHEYENNE

WI

MI

VT

NH

CA

• Denver

Kansas territory

IA

IL

IN

OH

NY

MA

CT RI

PA

Gila

New Mexico territory

unorganized territory

MO

36° 30'

KY

VA

NJ

DE

MD

Gadsden purchase

AR

TN

NC

TX

MS

AL

GA

SC

LA

FL

MEXICAN REPUBLIC

General Miramon in Mexico City

President Juarez in Vera Cruz

BAHAMAS (British)

LESSER ANTILLES

British   French

CUBA (Spanish)

DOMINICAN REP

HAITI

Slave states

JAMAICA (British)

PUERTO RICO (Spanish)

Belize (British)

November

1860

GUATEMALA

HONDURAS

opponent for some ill-chosen words on 'the crime against Kansas'. Though by 1858 the issue of Kansas had been settled, the consequences of the battle were still very much in evidence. The most important was the Republican Party.

The Republican Party, organized in 1854, was specifically set up to oppose the extension of slavery. Whereas most of the current crop of politicians hedged on this isssue because they realized that to be clear about it would foster the north–south polarization, the Republicans made it the central plank of their platform. They dismissed southern threats of boycott or secession as mere bluff. And in the 1856 presidential election the Republicans polled surprisingly well, gaining 38 percent of the presidential vote and carrying eleven northern states. In the mid-term election of 1858 they extended this electoral base. Events in Kansas and the pro-slavery decisions of the Supreme Court (the Dred Scott case, for example) had convinced a majority of people in the north that blocking the further spread of slavery had become a moral imperative.

Faced with this evidence of northern resolve, the leaders of the south reacted with the blind intransigence that characterized their actions throughout the later 1850s. The only hope of avoiding a head-on conflict lay with the Democratic Party, which had won the presidency for the old compromiser Buchanan in the last election and could very possibly win with Douglas, author of the Kansas–Nebraska act, in the next. But the deep south's delegates refused to support Douglas on the grounds that he had accepted the verdict of the Kansas referendum. They were so incensed by this 'betrayal' that they preferred to run a candidate of their own, John C. Breckinridge of Kentucky, even though this meant splitting the party. The political scene became even more confused when the border states lined up behind their idea of a compromise candidate, John Bell of Tennessee. As it turned out, the fact that the opposition to the Republican Party split three ways probably did not affect the result, for the south's extremism had so incensed the north that the Republican candidate

was able to carry all but one of the free states, and that was enough to ensure his election regardless of what happened south of the Mason–Dixon line.

The character of the Republican candidate undoubtedly played its part in this victory. Though Abraham Lincoln had not held any high political office he had, in a series of debates with Douglas in 1858, put the case for an end to compromise on slavery in the territories with an honesty and clarity that helped convince the party chiefs that this relative unknown from Illinois was the man to back. His performance in the election showed that their confidence was well founded. His next task was to justify his stand at the bar of history.

The United States was not the only country to undergo political polarization in the late 1850s. Mexican society was riven by an equally bitter conflict between liberals and conservatives. It began in 1855 when Mexico acquired what it had hitherto signally lacked, a genuinely reformist government. The liberals who dominated the new regime intended to start Mexico on the path of democracy by reducing the privileges of the landowners and encouraging the education of the masses. This brought them into conflict not just with the landowners but the Catholic Church. A counter-revolution mounted in 1858 forced the liberals from the capital but their following in the country at large enabled them to maintain their credibility as a government. Though General Miguel Miramon might rule in Mexico City, the liberal President Benito Juarez (a pure-blood Zapotec Indian, incidentally) maintained himself in Vera Cruz supported by the customs revenues of this important port. By late 1858, after three years of ebb and flow, the struggle was approaching its climax with General Miramon cooped up in Mexico City and liberal forces closing in from all directions. Miramon fought to the bitter end, but before the year was out he had been forced to flee both capital and country.

1 The long struggle over its constitution delayed the admission of Kansas till January 1861, too late for it to take part in the 1860 presidential election. Two new states that did make it in time are Minnesota, admitted to the Union in 1858, and Oregon, admitted in 1859. The territorial rearrangements involved in the creation of these two states deserve a brief mention. The lands in the western half of the old Minnesota territory were simply allowed to revert to the 'unorganized' category when the state was created out of the eastern half. The redistribution in the north-west went through two phases: the first saw the horizontal division of the Oregon territory with the creation of Washington territory in the north (1853); the second the splitting of the remainder into a western half (which became the State of Oregon) and an eastern half (added to Washington territory pro tem).

Of more moment than these temporary administrative shifts was the discovery of gold in the foothills of the Kansas territory (now Colorado) Rockies. The first strike was made in 1858: the consequence was a gold rush that brought 40,000 people into the area, and the mining town of Denver into existence, in the course of 1859. It also brought renewed trouble with the Indians, particularly the Cheyenne whose hunting grounds the would-be millionaires had to cross to reach their destination.

Finally note the creation of the Canadian province of British Columbia (1858), an administrative consequence of the Fraser river gold rush of the year before.

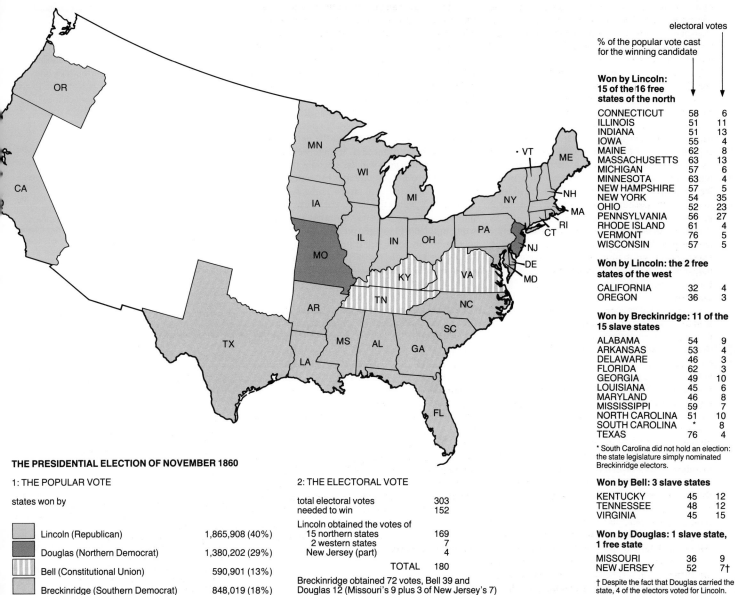

electoral votes

% of the popular vote cast
for the winning candidate

**Won by Lincoln:
15 of the 16 free
states of the north**

CONNECTICUT	58	6
ILLINOIS	51	11
INDIANA	51	13
IOWA	55	4
MAINE	62	8
MASSACHUSETTS	63	13
MICHIGAN	57	6
MINNESOTA	63	4
NEW HAMPSHIRE	57	5
NEW YORK	54	35
OHIO	52	23
PENNSYLVANIA	56	27
RHODE ISLAND	61	4
VERMONT	76	5
WISCONSIN	57	5

**Won by Lincoln: the 2 free
states of the west**

CALIFORNIA	32	4
OREGON	36	3

**Won by Breckinridge: 11 of the
15 slave states**

ALABAMA	54	9
ARKANSAS	53	4
DELAWARE	46	3
FLORIDA	62	3
GEORGIA	49	10
LOUISIANA	45	6
MARYLAND	46	8
MISSISSIPPI	59	7
NORTH CAROLINA	51	10
SOUTH CAROLINA	*	8
TEXAS	76	4

* South Carolina did not hold an election:
the state legislature simply nominated
Breckinridge electors.

Won by Bell: 3 slave states

KENTUCKY	45	12
TENNESSEE	48	12
VIRGINIA	45	15

**Won by Douglas: 1 slave state,
1 free state**

MISSOURI	36	9
NEW JERSEY	52	7†

† Despite the fact that Douglas carried the
state, 4 of the electors voted for Lincoln.

THE PRESIDENTIAL ELECTION OF NOVEMBER 1860

1: THE POPULAR VOTE

states won by

■	Lincoln (Republican)	1,865,908 (40%)
■	Douglas (Northern Democrat)	1,380,202 (29%)
▦	Bell (Constitutional Union)	590,901 (13%)
▨	Breckinridge (Southern Democrat)	848,019 (18%)

2: THE ELECTORAL VOTE

total electoral votes	303
needed to win	152

Lincoln obtained the votes of

15 northern states	169
2 western states	7
New Jersey (part)	4
TOTAL	**180**

Breckinridge obtained 72 votes, Bell 39 and
Douglas 12 (Missouri's 9 plus 3 of New Jersey's 7)

The most striking difference between this map and the last one showing the population of North and Central America, the map for 1750, is the increase in total numbers. Where there were 8.5 million people there are now 50 million. Almost equally striking is the shift in the demographic center of gravity. In 1750 the split in the continental total was two to one in favor of the area below the Rio Grande. Now the ratio is three to one in favor of the north. Where the earlier map showed a cluster of minor symbols restricted to the Atlantic seaboard we now have a spread of major ones – a million apiece – covering the whole area between the Mississippi and the Atlantic. The total adds up to 36 million. A century earlier it had been only 2 million.

One group conspicuously failed to share in this remarkable expansion. In 1860 there were actually fewer Indians north of the Rio Grande than there had been a century earlier: something of the order of 700,000 (500,000 in the USA, 200,000 in Canada) as against 800,000. Confined to the area west of the Mississippi, the red men could only wonder what depredations the next hundred years would bring.

A restricted distribution is also characteristic of North America's black population. The ante-bellum blacks were effectively confined to the slave states. Even the free blacks (perhaps 12 percent of the total) lived almost entirely in the south. Moreover, even within the slave states there was a strong southward bias to the distribution, with more than 60 percent living in the cotton belt, i.e., in the states between Texas in the west, and South Carolina in the east. This tier of six states (Texas, Louisiana, Mississippi, Alabama, Georgia and South Carolina), plus Florida, constituted the deep south – the realm of absolute intransigence on the slavery issue. By contrast the upper south – Missouri, Arkansas, Kentucky, Tennessee, North Carolina, Virginia, Maryland and Delaware – took a more moderate line. With fewer slaves and even fewer slave owners, they were unsure how far they should go in defense of the 'peculiar institution'. Should

they really put the preservation of slavery before the preservation of the Union?

The north saw little need for the south to search its heart so deeply. The Republican Party had no plans to abolish slavery, and President-elect Lincoln had been careful to distinguish between his public commitment to prevent any further extension of slavery and his private belief that the days of slavery itself were numbered. But back of Lincoln's appeal for calm was a confidence bred of his recent electoral victory and the nature of the forces that had produced it. If there were enough people in the north to win the election, there were enough to prevent any attempt by southerners to resist the collective will. Even if the southlands were united, which they were not, they contained only 8.5 million whites as against the 19 million living in the north. Moreover, the north had a far more vigorous and much faster growing economy. It has been reckoned that 90 percent of the business activity that took place in the United States at this time took place in the north.

But the deep south contained people who did not count the odds, men who had claimed for years that the only future for their society lay in a new nation separate from the United States. They saw the results of the election not as a warning to go carefully, but as a justification of their direst predictions and a spur to immediate action. No need to wait for Lincoln to take office, everyone knew the man was a sworn abolitionist. The south must be out of the Union before he became its president.

As always this sort of talk found its most enthusiastic audience in South Carolina, the state with the highest proportion of blacks (57 percent) and, doubtless because of this fact, the self-appointed champion of the southern lifestyle. As soon as the election of Lincoln had been confirmed the South Carolina legislature called a state convention which, on 20 December 1860, unanimously passed an 'ordinance of secession'. The links between South Carolina and the United States of America were formally dissolved, armed forces raised to resist any attempt by the Union govern-

ment to impose its authority and messengers dispatched to the other slave states demanding support. Obviously some of the southern states would have no compunction about going all the way with South Carolina. The questions all America was asking as 1860 drew to a close were which ones and how many? Would there be enough of them to give the breakaway movement a fighting chance?[1]

1 Although any analysis of the demographic changes in North and Central America in the period of 1750–1860 must necessarily have the United States as its main concern, developments in Canada, Mexico and the Caribbean deserve attention too. Canada's 1860 population of 3 million whites (indicated by symbols on Ontario, Quebec and New Brunswick) represents a massive 38-fold increase over the 1750 settlement. Most of this gain was due to immigration from Britain: as a result the proportion of French speakers fell from around 75% in 1750 to little more than 30% in 1860.

Mexico's population increase is remarkable for its modesty, for, by North American standards, 75 percent has to be counted as a very low figure. This relatively poor performance clearly reflects the social and economic stagnation characteristic of the country in the nineteenth century.

The changes in the Caribbean are more interesting. The late eighteenth-century revolt in St Domingue (subsequently Haiti) effectively eliminated the white population along with the slave economy. Much the same thing happened in the British islands when the decision was taken to abolish slavery in the 1830s. The white population dwindled, the black population which, in the days of slavery, had never been self-sustaining, began to expand and sugar exports collapsed. The story was repeated in the French islands after the abolition of slavery there in 1838. In one island, however, all these trends were reversed. This was Cuba which, in the early nineteenth century, became the world's leading exporter of sugar and continued to run an old-style plantation economy until well past the date of this map. Continuing immigration from Spain brought the white population up to 900,000 by 1860; continuing import of slaves from Africa (in defiance of the international ban on the Atlantic slave trade) brought the number of blacks up to 400,000. No wonder the Americans in the cotton belt looked on Cuba as a kindred state which would, if it could only be persuaded to make the break with Spain, make a useful reinforcement for the southern bloc.

SOUTH CAROLINA

Population in
December
1860

1,000,000
100,000

Indian

Mestizo

White

Mulatto

Black

The news of South Carolina's secession was greeted with enthusiasm throughout the deep south. One by one the states of the cotton belt declared that they too were leaving the Union, and early in February 1861 delegates from six of them (Texas was in agreement but unable to make it in time) met in Montgomery, Alabama, and set up a new organization, the Confederate States of America. The constitution of this body was modelled on that of the United States with, of course, the addition of special clauses in favor of slavery and states' rights. The post of president was conferred on Senator Jefferson Davis of Mississippi.

The creation of the Confederacy was a triumph for the extremist element in the south. It created a geographically solid bloc of seven states, enough to form a viable nation if given time to do so. What the politicians in Montgomery were not able to do was attract the support of the more moderate men who controlled the affairs of the upper south. The representatives of Arkansas, Tennessee, North Carolina and Virginia all refused to commit themselves at this stage for, dedicated as they were to the preservation of slavery and deeply distrustful as they might be of the north, they were not as yet ready to leave the Union. They would wait and see what President-elect Lincoln did when he took office.

In March, in one of the bleakest inaugurations in American history, Lincoln assumed the presidency. While making no specific threats, he made his position clear. The Union was indissoluble and, if necessary, force would be used to preserve it. On the other hand, there would be no rush to coercion. Perhaps the south would heed him when he said that he had no intention of interfering with the existing institution of slavery; maybe calmer councils would prevail and the rebellion could be ended without bloodshed. He hoped so. The tone was conciliatory, the reasoning firm, the effect nil. Everyone, north and south, had heard it all before.

If Lincoln was reluctant to take the first step –

and whether he was or not, he thought it important to appear so – everyone knew that the issue could not be postponed much longer. The United States Army, for example, maintained garrisons at four points in Confederate territory and all of these were in urgent need of resupply. In the case of Forts Jefferson and Taylor off the tip of Florida this posed no problem, for the government of Florida lacked the means to blockade them. Fort Pickens, in Pensacola Bay, was more vulnerable, but the US Navy was confident it could get supplies through if so ordered. The difficult one was Fort Sumter. Situated on an island in the middle of Charleston harbor, Sumter was ringed around by rebel batteries and, in a purely military sense, its relief would be hazardous in the extreme. It would also be very dangerous politically. South Carolina had already made it plain that it would regard any such move as an act of war.

In fact, Fort Sumter was a no-win situation. If it wasn't reprovisioned its supplies would give out in mid-April and its garrison would have to surrender. On the other hand, any attempt at reprovisioning, whether successful or not, would very likely bring down such a storm of shot and shell that the fort would be rendered untenable within a day or two. No wonder that Lincoln's cabinet advised him that the only practical thing to do was to bring the garrison out under flag of truce. It was inevitable that this would be seen as a victory for the Confederacy, but the Union could counter by presenting it as a victory for moderation, and at least the dignities would have been preserved.

Lincoln decided differently. In early April he ordered the US Navy to get supplies into Fort Sumter, by force if necessary. There was no attempt at secrecy, for the status quo in Charleston harbor had been preserved on the understanding that any convoy would be signalled in advance. Lincoln honored this agreement by sending a personal emissary to the Governor of South Carolina. The governor telegraphed the news to the Confederate government in Montgomery which, after some debate, decided to reduce the fort forthwith. The bombardment began early on the morning of

12 April. The Federal supply ships and their inadequate escort could only watch helplessly as the brick fort was pounded into rubble. Thirty-six hours after the opening shot, the garrison surrendered. The Confederacy had shown that it did not flinch from armed conflict.

Now it was Lincoln's turn to show equal determination. He issued an immediate call for 75,000 volunteers, confident that now the south had fired the first shot the north would respond in full measure. He was hopeful that the 'Upper South' would continue to stand aside and let the government take the steps necessary to maintain the Union. Because the Confederacy counted barely 5 of America's 30 million and more than 2 million of these were black slaves, the task did not seem insurmountable.

Unfortunately the bombardment of Fort Sumter aroused southern patriotism as strongly as northern. The day after Lincoln's call for volunteers went out Virginia voted eight-eight to fifty-three to join the Confederacy. No one doubted that North Carolina would follow Virginia's lead and it made the formal decision to do so in May. So did Arkansas and, in June, Tennessee. In the first four months of its existence the Confederacy had nearly doubled its strength.[1]

1 In the west note the admission of Kansas to the Union and the formation of two new territorial governments, Colorado and Dakota. In the Caribbean the decolonizing process has taken a step back with the return of the Spanish to Santo Domingo. The problems of the Dominican Republic had proved more than the local politicians could handle and they had decided to call on Spain to resume its colonial authority.

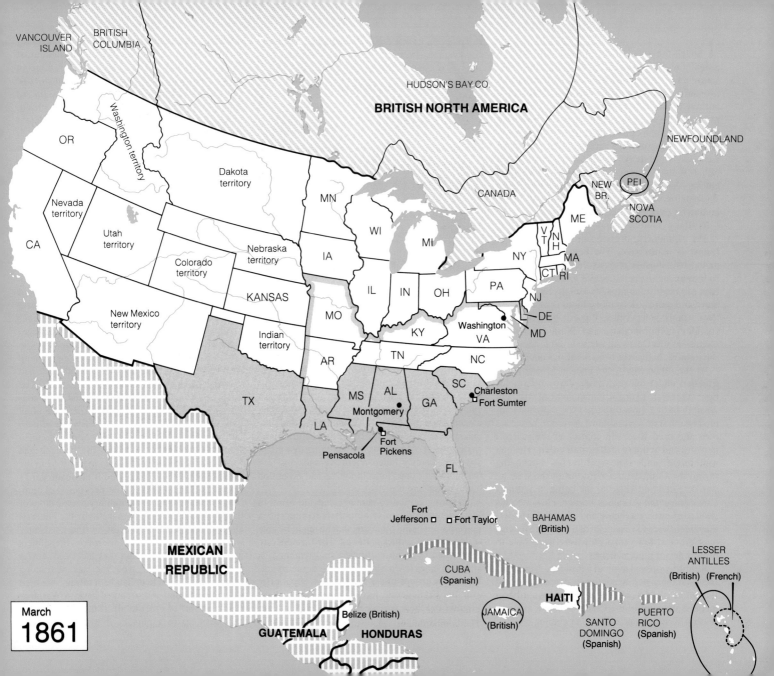

VANCOUVER ISLAND

BRITISH COLUMBIA

HUDSON'S BAY CO.

BRITISH NORTH AMERICA

NEWFOUNDLAND

CANADA

PEI

NOVA SCOTIA

NEW BR.

OR

Washington territory

Dakota territory

MN

ME

Nevada territory

Utah territory

CA

Colorado territory

Nebraska territory

IA

WI

MI

VT

NH

NY

MA

CT

RI

New Mexico territory

KANSAS

Indian territory

MO

IL

IN

OH

PA

NJ

DE

Washington

MD

VA

KY

TN

NC

AR

TX

MS

AL

SC

GA

Charleston
Fort Sumter

Montgomery

LA

Fort Pickens

Pensacola

FL

Fort Jefferson

Fort Taylor

BAHAMAS (British)

MEXICAN REPUBLIC

CUBA (Spanish)

HAITI

LESSER ANTILLES (British) (French)

JAMAICA (British)

SANTO DOMINGO (Spanish)

PUERTO RICO (Spanish)

Belize (British)

GUATEMALA

HONDURAS

March 1861

Though the middle rank of slave states had all joined the Confederacy by the spring of 1861, Lincoln was still hoping to keep the topmost line – Missouri, Kentucky, Maryland and Delaware – faithful to the Union. Indeed for the embattled president this was his most pressing concern during his first months in office. 'I hope to have God on my side,' he is reported as saying, 'but I must have Kentucky.' Yet there could be no certainty about either. With the Confederate flag flying over Alexandria, Virginia, just across the river from Washington, he could not even be sure of maintaining his position in the nation's capital.

Northern militia, responding to the call for 75,000 volunteers, proved sufficient to save the essentials in the east. The first regiments were pelted by a hostile mob as they passed through Baltimore and for a moment it looked as if Maryland too might renounce the Union. However, as more and more troops moved into the state from the north the voices calling for secession fell silent. By May both Maryland and Washington were secure – as was Delaware whose loyalty, despite its slave status, had never been in serious doubt.

At the other end of the line, in Missouri, the situation underwent an equally favorable resolution. General Lyon, commandant of the US Armory at St Louis, dispersed the militia assembled by the state's secessionist governor, raised his own and used it to win control of the railroad network and hence of all the vital centers. He then went further, indeed he went too far. Attempting to run the Confederates right out of the state he was defeated and killed at the battle of Wilson's Creek, near the Arkansas border. However, his good work survived this defeat. Though Confederate raiders were to cause a lot of trouble in Missouri over the next few years, they were never able to occupy any of it permanently.

Kentucky proved more of a problem. Here, too, the governor was a southern sympathizer and though he could hardly hope to take his northern-inclined state out of the Union he could, and did, declare Kentucky neutral in the coming conflict.

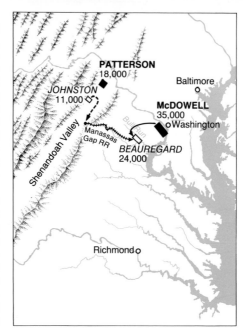

This was clever, for a neutral Kentucky was almost as valuable to the Confederacy as an openly pro-southern one. It acted as a shield for a long and vulnerable frontier and it prevented the Union commanders in the west from developing any meaningful strategy. Nor could this neutrality be challenged. To do so was the one thing that might drive the fiercely independent Kentuckians into the southern camp. Lincoln felt he had no option but to watch and wait.

As spring turned to summer and the army in Washington built up to respectable proportions Lincoln was possibly thinking that he might be able to do without Kentucky after all. The Confederate government was now installed in Richmond, a mere 125 miles to the south of the Federal capital. The Union troops had a three to two superiority over the Confederate forces defending northern Virginia and there was a good chance that a direct thrust at the heart of the rebel domain would

succeed. And if Richmond fell, the Confederacy might collapse before any significant amount of American blood had been spilt. In July Lincoln ordered General Irvin McDowell, commander of the Federal forces in Washington, to try it. McDowell duly took his army, 35,000 strong, across the Potomac and set out for the Confederate capital.

McDowell's army was not the only one on the board. A confederate force of 24,000 men commanded by General P. G. T. Beauregard, the victor of Fort Sumter, had recently taken up a defensive position behind Bull Run Creek, twenty-five miles down the Richmond road. And, forty miles to the north-west of the Bull Run position, in the Shenandoah Valley, another pair of armies faced each other, 18,000 men under Union General Robert Patterson and 11,000 under Confederate General J. E. Johnston. McDowell's assumption was that Patterson and Johnston would balance each other out, leaving him free to deal with Beauregard.

The Battle of Bull Run, the first major engagement of the Civil War, began promisingly for the Union side. McDowell marched his men round Beauregard's left flank and the Confederates had to make an awkward turn to meet his attack. The Union movement was well conceived and, considering the lack of training and experience of all concerned, surprisingly vigorously executed. Unfortunately McDowell's effort was doomed from the start because before the battle began Johnston had brought his command over from the Shenandoah valley and placed it at Beauregard's disposal. This gave the southerners parity of numbers which, in terms of the military practicalities of the day, made an offensive success by the Federals almost impossible. When the northern advance was brought to a halt in mid-afternoon, the soldiers quickly sensed that the task they had been set was beyond their strength. Now the lack of training began to tell. Unable to handle a retreat, the men just turned round and streamed back to Washington in no sort of order at all. If the Confederates had been up to a pursuit, it would have been

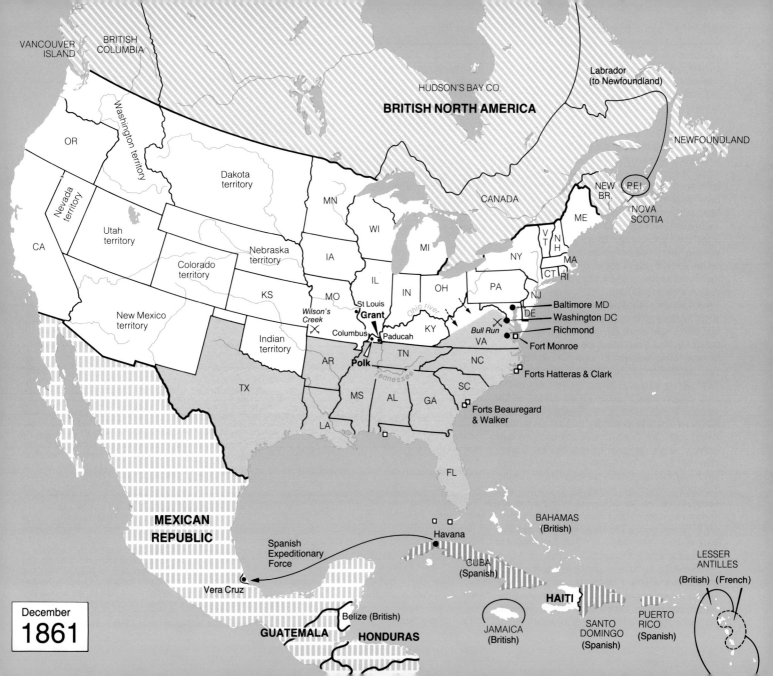

VANCOUVER ISLAND

BRITISH COLUMBIA

HUDSON'S BAY CO.

BRITISH NORTH AMERICA

Labrador (to Newfoundland)

NEWFOUNDLAND

OR

Washington territory

Dakota territory

CANADA

P.E.I.

NOVA SCOTIA

NEW BR.

ME

Nevada territory

Utah territory

MN

WI

MI

NY

VT
N
H

MA

CA

Nebraska territory

IA

IL

OH

PA

CT
RI

NJ

Colorado territory

KS

MO

IN

Ohio river

DE

Baltimore MD
Washington DC
Richmond
Fort Monroe

St Louis

Grant

KY

VA

New Mexico territory

Wilson's Creek

Columbus

Paducah

Bull Run

Indian territory

Polk

TN

Tennessee

NC

AR

NC

SC

Forts Hatteras & Clark

TX

MS

AL

GA

Forts Beauregard & Walker

LA

FL

MEXICAN REPUBLIC

BAHAMAS (British)

Spanish Expeditionary Force

Havana

Vera Cruz

CUBA (Spanish)

HAITI

LESSER ANTILLES

(British) (French)

Belize (British)

GUATEMALA

HONDURAS

JAMAICA (British)

SANTO DOMINGO (Spanish)

PUERTO RICO (Spanish)

December
1861

disastrous. As they were not, Bull Run was simply a humiliation. But in strategic terms the defeat was an important one: the chance of ending the war at a stroke had gone forever.

To rebuild the morale of the Federal forces in Washington, Lincoln brought in the one undoubted hero that the north had produced so far, General George B. McClellan. As commander of the Ohio militia, he had organized and executed an invasion of trans-Appalachian Virginia that had succeeded in detaching this territory from the Confederacy. Though most of the engagements had been small, they had all been Union victories and McClellan could reasonably take credit for the outcome of this important campaign. He certainly projected a good image. Everyone in Washington was sure that he would be able to repeat his success on the eastern side of the mountains and so bring the south to reason. There was even talk of him as America's next president.[1]

As Lincoln waited for McClellan to put the Army of the Potomac back on its feet, something McClellan said from the start he could not do before the New Year, he got the piece of good news he had most wanted to hear: Kentucky had declared for the Union. The decision followed a Confederate advance into the western end of the state and confirmed Lincoln in the wisdom of his watch-and-wait policy. Now the proud Kentuckians were actually asking for Federal protection. Better still, the Confederates did not gain any military advantage from making the first move. General Leonidas Polk's idea had been to forestall any Federal advance down the Mississippi or up the Tennessee rivers by occupying Columbus and Paducah. He got to Columbus all right but his opposite number on the Union side, General Ulysses S. Grant, reached Paducah before he did. Far from making Tennessee safer, Polk had opened it to Union attack.

Meanwhile, in Mexico a different sort of confrontation was taking place. The government of Benito Juarez was as honest a government as the country had known, but it was not able to cope with the financial mess left by years of misrule and civil strife. In particular it was not able to service its large foreign debt. The major creditors – Britain, France and Spain – met in London to discuss what should be done about this and decided that the answer was to send a naval expedition to Vera Cruz. The customs duties levied there, which amounted to half the revenue of the Mexican state, could be used to service the loans and pre-empting them in this way would encourage the Mexicans to put their house in order. The operation got off to a bloodless start in December 1861 when 6,000 Spaniards landed unopposed at Vera Cruz and occupied the town. It became truly multi-national three weeks later with the arrival of 3,000 French soldiers and a token force of British marines.

1 McClellan's campaign in west Virginia had the full support of the local population. The west Virginians had long resented the arrogance of their eastern compatriots who monopolized the state's offices and who always assumed that in speaking for the slave interest they were speaking for all Virginians. The war gave trans-Appalachian Virginia the opportunity to set up its own government. This was recognized by Lincoln, in the first instance as the lawful government of the entire state, then, more realistically, as the government of a new political unit, the state of West Virginia (1863). Some sorts of secession were acceptable even to Unionists.

West Virginia contained roughly one-third of Virginia's white population (350,000 out of a total of a little over a million) but, as might be expected from its politics, it had a much smaller proportion – less than a twentieth – of the state's 600,000 blacks.

Also to be noted are the first moves by the Union to make its maritime blockade of the south effective. An expedition in late August seized Forts Hatteras and Clark on the North Carolina coast and a second in early November took Forts Beauregard and Walker, the keys to Port Royal in South Carolina. The other east coast fort shown in Union hands, Fort Monroe at the tip of the Yorktown peninsula, had always been under Federal control.

By January 1862 the government of the United States had at its disposal armed forces of a magnitude undreamed of in peacetime. In less than twelve months the army had grown from 16,000 men to more than 600,000, which, in theory at least, was enough to carry out major operations on every front. Of course, the rebel Confederacy had its armies too. In the first year of its existence it had raised the remarkable total of a quarter of a million men and, even more remarkably, managed to equip most of them. Still, at every point that mattered, the Union forces outnumbered their opponents by better than two to one, and President Lincoln could not for the life of him understand why his generals were so reluctant to advance. At one White House dinner he was heard to remark that if General McClellan did not plan to use the Army of the Potomac, he would like to borrow it, though he hastened to add that someone would have to tell him what to do with it.

While McClellan was still explaining to everyone why he couldn't move forward, news arrived from the west that General Grant had done so. He had advanced up the Tennessee and reduced the only major defensive work the Confederates had on that river, Fort Henry. Then, turning east, he had marched his men the dozen miles to Fort Donelson on the Cumberland River. As the Cumberland led directly to Nashville, the capital of Tennessee, the Confederates felt bound to reinforce Fort Donelson and they duly did so, bringing the garrison up to a strength comparable to Grant's (21,000 v. 27,000). What they did not provide was leadership. The two top generals mishandled the defense, mishandled an attempted break-out and then fled, leaving the third in command to ask Grant for terms. 'No terms except unconditional and immediate surrender,' replied Grant, adding for good measure, 'I propose to move immediately upon your works.' Fort Donelson and 15,000 prisoners were in Union hands by noon the next day.

Grant now switched back to the Tennessee, leaving the occupation of Nashville to his col-

league, General Don Carlos Buell. The idea was for the two of them to combine their armies and advance on Corinth, a rail junction where the north–south Columbus to Mobile railroad (not shown) intersected the east–west Chattanooga to Memphis line on which the Confederate position on the central Mississippi depended. Grant moved ahead confidently, Buell trailed along after him; both discounted the possibility of the weakened Confederate forces launching a counter-offensive. But General A. S. Johnston, the Confederate commander in the west, had persuaded Jefferson Davis to make new forces available to him and he, too, could read the railroad map. He used all four lines leading to Corinth to obtain a concentration of 44,000 men, giving him a slight edge over Grant who was forming up at Shiloh, twenty miles to the north. Johnston also had the advantage of surprise. On 6 April he launched an all-out attack on Grant's army that forced one division to surrender and beat the rest back to their Tennessee landing-stage. But the Confederate forces, though apparently victorious, were hurt almost as badly and the balance tipped against them with the arrival of Buell's vanguard during the night. Outnumbered 55,000 to 35,000, General Beauregard, who had succeeded to the Confederate command when Johnston received a mortal wound, reluctantly pulled away from the battlefield. The Union forces, considerably sobered, took the better part of the next two months to complete their programmed advance on Corinth.

Meanwhile, McClellan had unveiled his strategy for winning the war. Instead of trying to fight his way along the road to Richmond he would ship his army to the Yorktown Peninsula and move on the Confederate capital from there. This would reduce the distance the army would have to march from the 120 miles that separated Richmond from Washington to a mere sixty, with a corresponding alleviation of the tactical and supply problems involved. Lincoln approved the plan with the proviso that sufficient troops be left behind to safeguard Washington. In early April McClellan landed in the peninsula and began operations. It

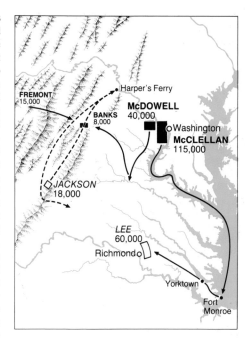

was the sort of campaigning that suited him, a slow, methodical advance that brought his army to the outskirts of Richmond by the end of May. As he had 100,000 men to the Confederates' 50,000, the fall of the city seemed only a matter of time.

In this crisis of the Confederacy Jefferson Davis turned to his most trusted military adviser, General Robert E. Lee. Assuming direct command of the forces defending Richmond, Lee had his men dig in and thin out along the southern three-quarters of the front so that the bulk of them could be concentrated at its northern end. He also called in Stonewall Jackson's army which had been charging up and down the Shenandoah valley to such good effect that Lincoln, despite McClellan's repeated pleas for reinforcements, felt unable to release any of the 70,000 men he had retained for the defense of Washington. Lee deployed Jackson's forces on the left too. This gave him a three to two advantage over McClellan's right wing (though the Union

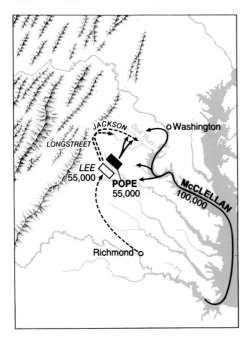

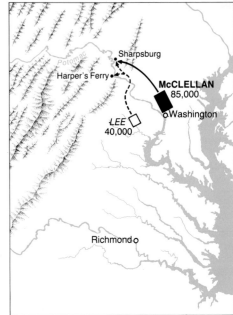

ordered him to pull his forces out of the peninsula and re-deploy them in support of Pope.

Alas, Lincoln was no strategist. His well-meant initiative gave Lee the opportunity of defeating Pope before McClellan's troops could be on the field again, and Lee wasn't the man to pass up this sort of chance. He slipped Jackson's corps round the right flank of Pope's army and onto its supply line. Then, when Pope turned to deal with Jackson, he appeared alongside his lieutenant with his entire army. The two sides clashed on the old Bull Run battlefield and the story was much the same as the year before. The Union Army attacked with great *élan* but took such heavy losses that eventually the fight went out of it. This time the retreat to Washington was reasonably disciplined, but the humiliation was just as great. After a year's campaigning the Army of the Potomac was back at its starting-point, with nothing to show for its efforts but a long casualty list and a brace of discredited generals. Lincoln relieved Pope of his command and, swallowing hard, gave McClellan the job of restoring the army's morale. There seemed to be nobody else to turn to.

There were two more battles in the east before the year was out. In September Lee crossed the Potomac with the intention of moving the war onto Union ground and, if there was a favorable opportunity, trouncing its forces again. It was risky, for his men were exhausted and only 40,000 of them followed him north. Worse still, his plan of campaign fell into McClellan's hands within a few days of the start of the operation. Knowing where to find Lee, McClellan was able to bring more than 80,000 men against him, and it was Lee who stood on the defensive in the battle that followed. Named alternatively after Antietam Creek, or Sharpsburg town, this was to be the bloodiest single day's fighting of the entire war. Repeated, if poorly coordinated, Union attacks nearly broke the Confederate line on several occasions but the end result was a tactical standoff. Lee held the field for twenty-four hours before withdrawing. The fact that he did so gave McClellan a technical victory and the Union Army a useful boost to its self-

forces still outnumbered him three to two overall) and Lee used this to launch a series of attacks which gradually crumpled up the Union line. The cost was high, for at the end of a week of battle (made famous as the Seven Days) the Confederates counted 20,000 casualties to the Union's 15,000 but McClellan had been driven back down the peninsula and Richmond had been saved. Almost as important, Lee had acquired an ascendancy over the Union forces that he was now to put to good use.

With McClellan beaten, Lincoln saw that the only hope of retrieving the campaign was to use the Washington-based army offensively. He entrusted it to General Pope, who had the reputation of being an energetic commander, and ordered it south. He also sent instructions to McClellan to support Pope's operation by resuming the offensive himself. McClellan, convinced he was outnumbered, refused to move unless reinforced. Lincoln, finally losing patience with 'America's Napoleon',

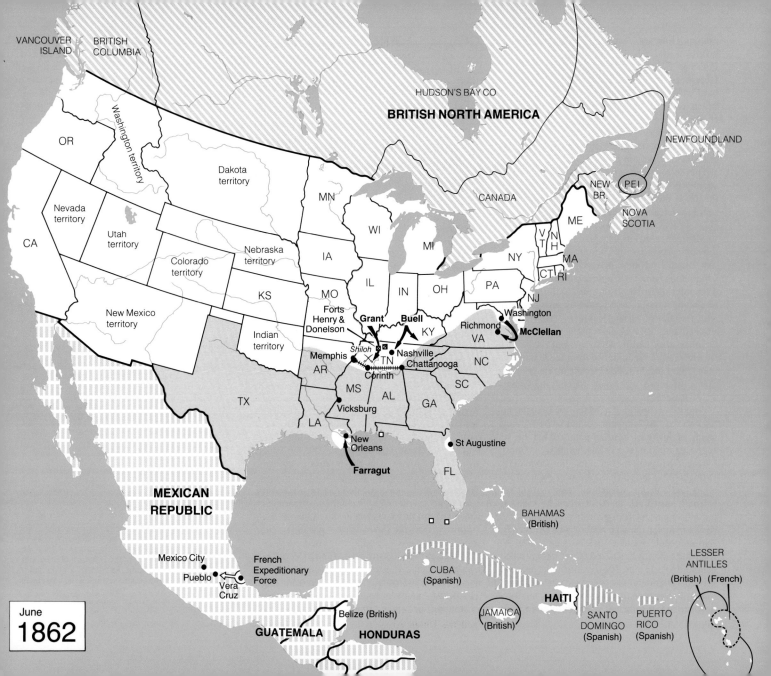

VANCOUVER ISLAND

BRITISH COLUMBIA

HUDSON'S BAY CO

BRITISH NORTH AMERICA

NEWFOUNDLAND

OR

Washington territory

Dakota territory

CANADA

NEW BR.

PEI

NOVA SCOTIA

Nevada territory

Utah territory

MN

WI

MI

ME

VT N H

NY

MA

CT RI

CA

Colorado territory

Nebraska territory

IA

IL

IN

OH

PA

NJ

New Mexico territory

KS

MO

Forts Henry & Donelson

Grant **Buell**

KY

Washington

Richmond

McClellan

VA

Indian territory

Shiloh

Memphis

TN

Nashville
Chattanooga

NC

AR

Corinth

SC

MS

AL

GA

TX

Vicksburg

LA

New Orleans

St Augustine

Farragut

FL

MEXICAN REPUBLIC

BAHAMAS (British)

CUBA (Spanish)

LESSER ANTILLES

(British) (French)

Mexico City

Pueblo

Vera Cruz

French Expeditionary Force

JAMAICA (British)

HAITI

SANTO DOMINGO (Spanish)

PUERTO RICO (Spanish)

Belize (British)

GUATEMALA **HONDURAS**

June
1862

esteem. However, Antietam was far from being a historical watershed. When the Army of the Potomac headed south again, which it did in December, it suffered its worst defeat yet. The battle of Fredericksburg was a one-sided affair in which General Burnside, the man Lincoln had chosen to succeed McClellan, made a rash attempt to bulldoze Lee's army out of a well-prepared defensive position. The Union forces took 12,000 casualties for no gain at all.

The second half of the year proved almost equally disappointing in the west though in this theater it was a matter of stagnation rather than outright defeat. After taking Corinth, Grant and Buell went their separate ways, Grant turning west to Memphis which he occupied in June, and Buell moving eastward with Chattanooga as his objective. Buell's advance petered out just short of Chattanooga and the Confederates then mounted a counter-offensive from this and their other remaining bases in east Tennessee, striking north with the aim of raising Kentucky. They did not succeed and, after a drawn battle at Perryville in October, they had to withdraw, but they had so clearly wrested the initiative from the Union command that Lincoln decided to replace Buell with an officer of more aggressive reputation, General W. S. Rosecrans.

Grant's occupation of Memphis brought him back to the Mississippi at a point some 150 miles south of his 1861 starting-point. What he was supposed to do next was join hands with Admiral Farragut in front of the one remaining Confederate stronghold on the river, Vicksburg. Admiral Farragut had got this Mississippi campaign off to a splendid start back in April when he sailed his battlefleet past the forts guarding the mouth of the river and forced the surrender of New Orleans. But Farragut could not take Vicksburg by himself – he tried and failed in June – and Grant was not able to get there to help him. The logistics of the operation proved insurmountable and the year ended with him still trying to find a way to get his forces downstream in sufficient strength to place Vicksburg under formal siege.

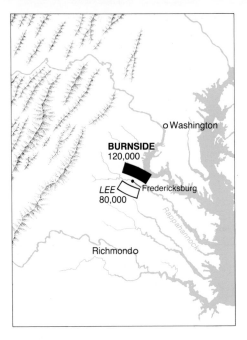

So 1862 drew to a close with the battle lines showing little change since the spring. The struggle had been harder and the casualty lists longer than anyone had expected, but neither side was discouraged. On the contrary, the easy enthusiasms of the early days had been replaced by a grim determination to see the struggle through. The hardening attitude was reflected in the politics of the war which had acquired a momentum of their own. There was to be no more fudging of the slavery issue. In September Lincoln's Preliminary Emancipation Proclamation declared that as from 1 January 1863 all slaves in the seceding states would, 'henceforward and forever, be free'.[1]

In Mexico the tripartite occupation of Vera Cruz became a purely French operation with the departure of the British and Spanish in April 1862. The British had never been interested in anything except getting their money back, while the Spanish, who had considered intervening in favor

of the local Conservatives, finally decided not to get mixed up in Mexican politics. The French, on the other hand, reckoned that they could and should install a Conservative government, something on the lines of the revived Napoleonic Empire currently established in France. With this in mind they built up their expeditionary force to 6,000 men and set out for Mexico City. They got no further than Puebla, where a surprisingly stout Mexican defense convinced them that more troops would be needed if they were to carry out their plans. After due consideration, France's Emperor Napoleon III decided to make the extra men available.

1 The Union blockade of the Confederate coastline became increasingly effective in the course of 1862. The US Navy used its command of the Hatteras inlet to mount a series of operations within the North Carolina Sounds which had sealed off this entire section of the coast by the beginning of the summer. Farragut's seizure of New Orleans gave the Union a commanding position in the Gulf; minor operations resulted in the capture of the old Spanish post at St Augustine, Florida.

The Federal government's strategy for 1863 followed the plan laid down the year before. General Grant was supposed to take Vicksburg, and General Rosecrans drive forward from Nashville via Chattanooga to Atlanta. Then the two western armies would join the Army of the Potomac in a concentric attack on the heartland of the Confederacy, Virginia and the Carolinas. That should be enough to bring the war to a speedy conclusion. Of course there was always the chance that the Army of the Potomac would get to Richmond and extinguish the rebellion unaided, but somehow that did not seem very likely. The scoreboard for encounters between the Confederate and Union forces in Virginia stood at Confederates 4, Federals 0, and few people felt that the Army of the Potomac had the measure of Lee's Army of Northern Virginia.

One person who would have disputed this assessment was Joe Hooker, the Army of the Potomac's new commander and a man of boundless self-confidence. That he could lead the Union's forces to victory he never doubted; the question was what would he do next? President of the United States? Dictator for life? The possibilities were limitless. Lincoln did his best to bring Hooker down to earth. He pointed out that he had given him the job in spite of, not because of his big mouth, and went on to observe: 'Only those generals who gain successes can set up as dictators. What I ask of you is military success, and I will risk the dictatorship.'

News of a battle won by General Rosecrans started the new year off on a good note. Moving out of Nashville in the last days of 1862, Rosecrans had encountered the Confederate Army of Tennessee under General Braxton Bragg at Stone's River, a few miles short of Murfreesboro. A hard-fought engagement spread over four days had ended in Confederate defeat and Rosecrans was now the master of Murfreesboro town. So ran the official report and as far as the outcome is concerned it was essentially true. What Rosecrans left out was that he had been surprised and very nearly beaten in a battle that had many points of resem-

blance to Shiloh. Just how heavily the Union army had been punished became apparent as the months passed and Rosecrans refused point-blank to move beyond Murfreesboro.

General Grant did better. After an exceptionally frustrating period in which he found he could not get at Vicksburg from the north or west he finally worked out a plan for doing so from the south and east. This meant cutting himself off from his supply line which in turn meant that he had to obtain a decisive success within two weeks of his starting date. This he proceeded to do. From his landing point thirty miles south of Vicksburg Grant struck east to take Jackson, the Mississippi state capital, in a move that not only demoralized the Confederate command but also cut Vicksburg off from any hope of relief. Then he swung back to the Mississippi, took the bluffs north of Vicksburg and re-established his supply line. His attempt to take Vicksburg by storm was bloodily repulsed, but the siege lines he then drew round the city guaranteed its eventual capture.

While Grant was bringing the Mississippi campaign to its culmination, the Army of the Potomac was experiencing its usual vicissitudes. Towards the end of April Joe Hooker decided that the time had come to make good on his boasts and dispose of Lee for good and all. The first step was to finesse him out of the defensive position he was occupying at Fredericksburg. Hooker proposed to do this by gripping Lee's right and marching round his left, a maneuver which entailed dividing the Union Army into two. It looked a bit dangerous on paper but Hooker, with 130,000 men to Lee's 60,000, felt that there was no reason to expect any problems. No reason except previous experience. Lee split his army three ways, left one force to hold Fredericksburg, used the second to slow Hooker's advance, and sent Stonewall Jackson with the third on a circular march round the Union right. Hooker, who had proved surprisingly hesitant in his handling of the Confederate forces facing him, went to pieces completely when Jackson's veterans, rebel yells and all, came charging in on his right. The battle (named after Chancellorsville,

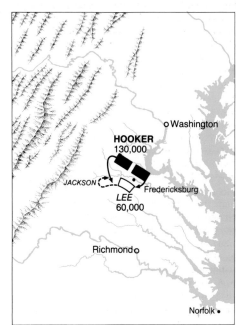

95

ten miles west of Fredericksburg) became a Confederate victory because Hooker – 'Fighting Joe', as he liked to be known – sounded the retreat.

What happened next has to be seen in the context of Chancellorsville. Lee decided to take the offensive and strike into Pennsylvania. The Army of the Potomac, now under the command of General George Meade, came up behind him and the two sides fought an unplanned three-day battle at Gettysburg. For the first two days Lee had the better of it, driving the Union troops back onto the defensive and pressing them hard on both flanks. On the morning of the third day he was confident that all that was needed for victory was a full-blooded thrust at the Union center. He massed his guns, brought up his one remaining division of fresh troops, Pickett's Virginians, and put them at the head of an assault wave 15,000 strong. It was nowhere near enough. Pickett's charge was broken well before it touched the Union line. Lee had wildly overestimated the degree to which he could bully the Army of the Potomac.

Despite its bruising repulse and its 33 percent casualty list, Lee's Army of Northern Virginia remained a formidable force. General Meade, looking out across the corpse-strewn battlefield, had no intention of putting his successful action at risk by going over to the offensive, and for the rest of that day and most of the next the Union army kept to its lines. Only then – late on the afternoon of 4 July – did it become clear that the Confederates were in retreat and that Gettysburg had been a major Union victory. The news, telegraphed to Washington, gave Lincoln the best Independence Day of his presidency.

Just how good it had been only became apparent three days later when the Navy reported that the Union flag was now flying over Vicksburg. Grant had taken the city and 30,000 prisoners, the biggest haul of the war. A few days more and the last Confederate post on the Mississippi, Fort Hudson, struck its colors too. Lincoln was able to report to Congress that 'The Father of Waters again goes unvexed to the sea.'

At long last everything seemed to be going right.

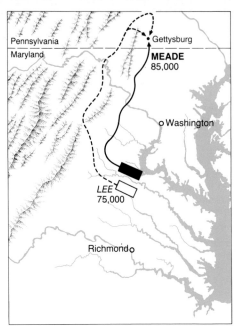

Even General Rosecrans, who had appeared to be turning into a second McClellan, was moving forward again. Leading the Army of the Cumberland out of Murfreesboro at the end of June, he consistently outmaneuvered his opponent, General Bragg, forcing him step by step back to Chattanooga. The town, a major Union objective for more than a year, fell in early September, enabling a jubilant Rosecrans to announce that he was now going on to Atlanta. What Rosecrans did not know was that Jefferson Davis had been so alarmed by the news from the west – first Vicksburg, now Chattanooga – that he had ordered every available reinforcement despatched to Bragg. He had even persuaded Lee to release Longstreet's veteran corps, one of the most important units in the Army of Northern Virginia. As a result, when Rosecrans emerged from Chattanooga the odds were tipping against him. Sensing that something was wrong he managed to pull his

widely spread corps together in time for the battle that began at Chickamauga Creek, ten miles south of the town, but his line was disorderly and he had to keep shifting the individual divisions around during the course of the fighting. One such move on the second day brought disaster, opening a gap in the Union line at the very time and place that Longstreet had chosen for his attack. The Union right collapsed, the men streaming back to Chattanooga in total rout. The left, commanded by imperturbable General George Thomas, held through that day and then fell back on Chattanooga too. As Bragg moved forward to besiege the town, a highly alarmed Lincoln began looking for ways to succor the Army of the Cumberland which Rosecrans reported was too weak to break out.

The means were ready to hand. Two corps were detached from the Army of the Potomac and a third, Sherman's, was ordered over from Vicksburg. Most important of all, Grant was put in command. By late November Grant had everything ready for the relief of Chattanooga and this he quickly achieved, knocking Bragg out of position and twenty miles down the road to Atlanta. Chickamauga, the Confederacy's one offensive success of the year, proved a sterile victory.[1]

In March 1863 the French Army in Mexico which had been built up to a strength of 35,000 men, had a second try at Puebla. This time it was successful, the city falling after a two-month siege, and success at Puebla opened the way to Mexico City. The leading French corps entered the capital in early June, the conservatives and clerics rallied in support of the French plan to turn Mexico into a monarchy. By September the country had two rival governments, a republican one under Juarez, now relocated in San Luis Potosi, and a French-protected regency in Mexico City. On the advice of the French the regents decided to offer the vacant throne to Maximilian, younger brother of the Emperor of Austria.

1 Changes in the political map of the United States during this period include the creation of the state of West Virginia and the organization of the Arizona and Idaho territories.

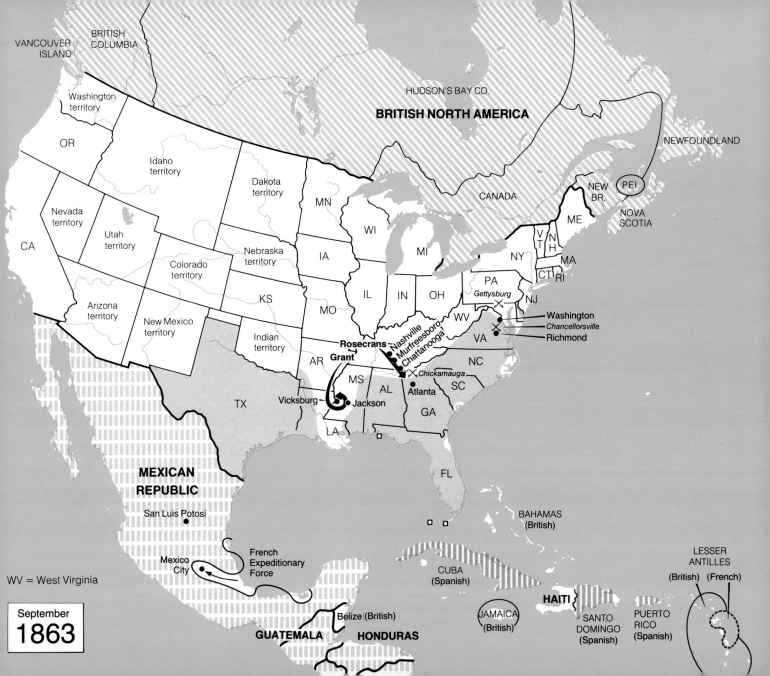

VANCOUVER ISLAND

BRITISH COLUMBIA

Washington territory

OR

Nevada territory

CA

Utah territory

Arizona territory

New Mexico territory

Idaho territory

Colorado territory

Dakota territory

Nebraska territory

KS

Indian territory

MN

WI

IA

MO

AR

TX

LA

MEXICAN REPUBLIC

San Luis Potosi

Mexico City

French Expeditionary Force

HUDSON'S BAY CO.

BRITISH NORTH AMERICA

NEWFOUNDLAND

CANADA

PEI

NEW BR.

NOVA SCOTIA

ME

MI

NY

VT

NH

MA

CT

RI

PA

Gettysburg

NJ

WV

Gettysburg ✕

✕ Washington

Chancellorsville

✕ Richmond

VA

IL

IN

OH

Rosecrans Nashville Murfreesboro Chattanooga

Grant

NC

✕ *Chickamauga*

SC

MS

AL

Atlanta

GA

Vicksburg ~ Jackson

FL

BAHAMAS (British)

Belize (British)

GUATEMALA

HONDURAS

CUBA (Spanish)

JAMAICA (British)

HAITI

SANTO DOMINGO (Spanish)

PUERTO RICO (Spanish)

LESSER ANTILLES (British) (French)

WV = West Virginia

September
1863

In March 1864 Congress revived the rank of lieutenant-general, in abeyance since the retirement of its sole previous holder, George Washington. President Lincoln was pleased to hear this. It showed the widespread support that existed for a move he had already decided on, the elevation of General Grant to supreme command of all the Union's armies and the co-ordination under his authority of the offensive operations planned for the year.

The co-ordination turned out to be somewhat less than perfect. Grant wanted the army based on the Lower Mississippi to advance eastward against Mobile, Alabama, a move that would bring it into the main theater of operations again. He was disappointed to find that it was already committed to a drive up the Red River, an enterprise of purely local significance, and that it was too late to get its orders changed. Nevertheless, Grant was able to exert full control over the movements planned for the two main Union armies: the Army of the Potomac, which was to get to grips with General Lee, and Sherman's army, which was to advance from Chattanooga to Atlanta and bring the war to the as yet untouched heartland of the Confederacy. In the first week of May both these armies moved out of their bivouacs, General Grant accompanying the Army of the Potomac, of which he became the effective commander.

Grant's lead column made contact with Lee's forces just west of Chancellorsville in a densely thicketed area known as the Wilderness. The two sides tumbled into battle barely able to see what they were doing, and a vicious series of attacks and counter-attacks followed one another over this and the next day. Every Union attempt to advance was thwarted and eventually mounting casualties forced Grant to abandon the offensive. By being quicker on their feet and more adept at finding flanking positions, Lee and the Army of Northern Virginia had, as usual, managed to get the better of their opponents. For the Federals, both officers and men, it was a bitter disappointment. They had looked for great things from Grant, but he had

turned out no different from the other generals who had led out the Army of the Potomac and then had to lead it back again. The orders to abandon their hard-won positions in the Wilderness were received in a mood of weary resignation.

But this time it was not quite the mixture as before. At the first crossroads that they came to, the Federal columns were met by the commander-in-chief, Ulysses S. Grant no less, standing by the side of the road and pointing, not north to Washington, but south to Richmond. In later years veterans of the Army of the Potomac would swear to this story, would tell anyone who would listen how they had seen old Grant standing there, with his hat pushed back and his cheroot in his hand, and go on to recall how the men had cheered and the marching pace had picked up as regiment after regiment made that right turn and tramped off into the dusk. Maybe it was really like this. Grant was certainly somewhere in the area at the time, he was surely responsible for the army's orders and there was, no doubt of it, a deal of cheering as the staff officers galloped about supervising the change of direction. For, whatever else happened, it was on this night and in this place that the Army of the Potomac found what it had been looking for for so long, a general who was not going to be put down by Robert E. Lee.

The next step on the road to Richmond was Spotsylvania Court-House and with a head start the Union forces ought to have been there before the Confederates. But the Army of the Potomac, even under Grant's direction, was still apt to under-perform, never going quite as far or as fast as its orders called for. By contrast, once Lee realized what was happening, the troops he sent off to match the Federal move did him proud. By marching through the night they got to the Spotsylvania crossroads first. Grant would have to fight to get the position he wanted.

The struggle that followed was every bit as ferocious as the battle in the Wilderness. The Confederates, aiming to do no more than deny Spotsylvania Court-House to the Federals, had the easier task, but a massive Union assault on the fifth

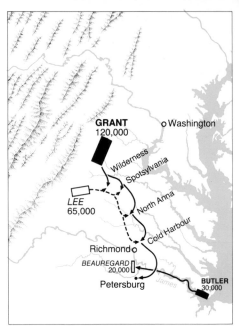

day broke the center of their line and brought Grant within an ace of victory. To restore the situation Lee had to organize a counter-attack, and to ensure its success he decided to lead it himself, something he had never considered necessary before. The soldiers would not have it. They sent him to the rear, fought the Federals to a standstill and saved the day. But though the Army of Northern Virginia managed to thwart Grant tactically, it could not put him off his strategic aim. One by one he shifted his corps to the east of Spotsylvania and sent them marching south again.

Twice more the Army of Virginia managed to interpose itself between Grant and Richmond, once at the North Anna River, where Grant simply backed off and went round, and again at Cold Harbor, where he tried to go through. This was a mistake. In less than thirty minutes the Union Army took 7,000 casualties and gained not a yard. Critics of Grant were quick to point out that this brought the butcher's bill for the five-week campaign to a staggering 50,000 and that despite this unprecedented loss the Army of the Potomac was no closer to Richmond than it had been two years earlier under McClellan.

The difference between the two occasions was none the less total. Grant had recovered the strategic authority that McClellan had lost. In the Seven Days it was the Army of Northern Virginia that had done all the attacking. Now Lee was reduced to following Grant about and fighting defensively. This was clearly shown when Grant moved on from Cold Harbor, crossed the James and made a thrust at Petersburg. The idea was to cut Richmond's communications with the south and, because Petersburg was stoutly defended, it did not work. But it demonstrated that Grant no longer had to worry about what Lee might do. He could leave the road to Washington wide open in the confidence that the Confederate Army was in no condition to take it.

While the Army of the Potomac marched and fought its way from the Wilderness to Petersburg, Sherman was leading the Armies of the West down the road from Chattanooga to Atlanta. The distance was comparable but the terrain was more difficult and the journey took longer. It was not till early July that the Union commander arrived before Atlanta and was able to place the city under formal siege. His opponent, General John Hood, made an aggressive and determined defense but, by swinging south and attacking the railroad on which the Confederate garrison depended for its supplies, Sherman was able to force Atlanta's evacuation in early September.

This was especially welcome news for Lincoln, who was up for re-election and badly needed a victory. He could not look to Grant, for though the lieutenant-general might have the Army of Northern Virginia where he wanted it, he had not been able to defeat it, nor take Richmond or even Petersburg, Sherman's seizure of Atlanta, plus a notable success by Union General Philip Sheridan in the Shenandoah valley, gave Republican campaign managers the morale-booster for which

they had been looking. When the votes were counted Lincoln had his second term by the handsome plurality of 212 electoral votes to twenty-one.

The sequel to the fall of Atlanta showed the degree to which the Union now had the upper hand. Sherman decided to ignore Hood, ignore his own lines of communication and march across Georgia to the eastern seaboard. Many prophesied that he would never make it, that without supplies his army would simply wither away, just as Napoleon's had during the Russian campaign. But so far from being a disaster, Sherman's progress was positively triumphal. His men found good pickings everywhere and, in the absence of significant opposition, were able to help themselves to anything they needed. And what they did not need they destroyed, on direct orders from their commander. They tore up the railroads, blew up the bridges, burned the houses of anyone who objected, and put an end to the plantation economy by freeing the slaves. Georgia was effectively knocked out of the war.

Sherman reached the coast at Savannah, which he was pleased to offer to President Lincoln as a Christmas present. Lincoln, who had had his doubts about the wisdom of Sherman's strategy (for that matter, so had Grant), was visibly relieved to hear that the Army of the West was once again safely in view. He was also very pleased to accept Sherman's Christmas gift. Savannah made a fine pair with Nashville, where Hood, who had tried to emulate Sherman's calculated daring by a foolhardy invasion of Tennessee, had come to grief at the hands of George Thomas. Hood's defeat was truly catastrophic. Of the 50,000 men who followed him into Tennessee less than 10,000 made it back to the south.

The New Year came and the Confederate flag still flew over Richmond. Jefferson Davis held his cabinet meetings as usual and delegates from the seceding states debated the measures the president placed before them. But the Confederacy, whose affairs they were supposed to be conducting, was visibly failing. Many of the areas that still remained faithful to the southern cause had been cut off from

the parent body by the Union offensives of the preceding two years. Contact with the outside world had been lost as a result of the Federal Navy's ever-tightening blockade. It was just possible to keep Lee's army supplied while it remained on the defensive, but raising a new army capable of stopping Sherman was out of the question. Yet if Sherman was not stopped he was bound to move north and join his army to Grant's, and once he did that Lee would be facing odds of three to one, more than even he could handle. There seemed only one solution to the manpower shortage and that was to arm the slaves. That in turn meant freeing them, which made the whole conflict absurd, but the logic of the moment demanded it; Lee pressed for it, and the Confederate Congress accepted it. The south would go down fighting, even if it was no longer clear what it was fighting for.

Sherman left Savannah at the beginning of February 1865. He took Columbia, capital of South Carolina, and more by design than by accident burnt most of it to the ground. Then he struck north again. President Lincoln, sensing that the end was near, moved down to Grant's headquarters where, to save unnecessary loss, he suggested postponing any assault on Petersburg until Sherman arrived. Grant thought otherwise. The Army of the Potomac, he said, had earned the right to make one last push for victory. For months the Union forces had been extending their lines in front of Petersburg, sometimes to the north to threaten Richmond, sometimes to the west to threaten the last railroad connection between Petersburg and the south. Lee had managed to match each move but his men were stretched very thin. Now Grant sent Sheridan with a strong force of infantry and cavalry to threaten that railroad again.

Lee reacted as strongly as he could, ordering out Pickett's division, the same that had led the famous charge at Gettysburg, later apostrophized as 'the high watermark of the Confederacy'. Now Pickett was to fight the Confederacy's last battle – and lose it. Sheridan was too quick and too strong for him, and the southerners were simply swept from the field. The next day the Army of the Potomac

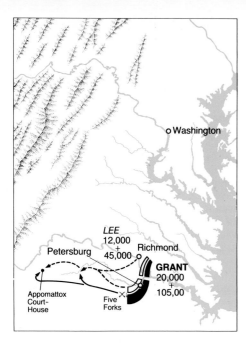

LEE
12,000
+
45,000

GRANT
20,000
+
105,00

Washington

Petersburg   Richmond

Appomattox
Court-
House

Five
Forks

stormed into Petersburg, bringing the ten-month siege to a close in six hours of furious fighting.

With Petersburg gone Lee had to evacuate Richmond. He gave orders that all stores that could not be moved should be set alight and by the time the last of his troops left the doomed city, the fires were raging out of control. So was the mob. The wretched inhabitants endured a night of terror before dawn came and the first Union troops moved in. Not far behind came Abraham Lincoln, a dozen armed sailors and a troop of jubilant blacks acting as escort. He did not say a great deal, just had a look round, visited Jefferson Davis's office and sat in his chair for a while. Military opinion suggested that Lee would probably surrender now 'if the thing be pressed'. Lincoln responded with a laconic telegram to Grant: 'Let the thing be pressed.'

Lee had left Richmond hoping that it would be possible to find a new base from which to continue

the war. First he tried to go south, only to have Sheridan get ahead of him and force him west. Then, a few days later, he found Sheridan in front of him again, and this time there was no way to turn. He wrote Grant for terms and the two met at Appomattox Court-House, where Grant agreed to Lee's men being paroled. As they laid down their arms and trudged off to their farms, the Army of Northern Virginia ceased to exist. Effectively the Civil War, the War between the States, the War for the Union, was over.

In practice it would take more than a month to call in all the soldiers and put an end to the fighting, and during that period many men were to die. Among them was Abraham Lincoln, assassinated by a vengeful southerner shortly after his return to Washington. The United States had to steer its way through the shoals of reconstruction without his guiding hand, but the loss has to be placed in the perspective of an achievement whose dimensions were already partly perceived: the Union had been preserved, and government of the people, by the people and for the people had been sustained.

The final eighteen months of the American Civil War saw Maximilian's Mexican Empire making steady progress. The republican forces were driven back into the extremities of the country and at every point where the French Army made a determined thrust it was able to substitute the writ of Mexico City for that of Chihuahua, the seat of the fugitive republican regime. Maximilian, who had arrived from Europe in May 1864, realized that at this stage he was bound to be entirely dependent on French bayonets. However, he hoped to achieve an independent role in due course by making himself the arbiter of conservative and liberal factions. To anyone who knew Mexico this seemed an implausible ambition but then Maximilian's hold on reality was fitful. Most of his waking hours were devoted to the production of a manual of court ceremonial which took 300 pages and twenty diagrams to solve problems of amazing irrelevance.[1]

1 In the western United States the year 1864 saw the admission of Nevada to the Union, the creation of the territory of Montana and a war with the southern Cheyenne brought on by the murder of a settler family near Denver. The Cheyenne war is remembered nowadays for the Sand Creek massacre in which the Colorado militia shot down some 200 Indian men, women and children who had assembled under a flag of truce. This broke the power of the tribe whose surviving members were resettled in Indian territory the following year.

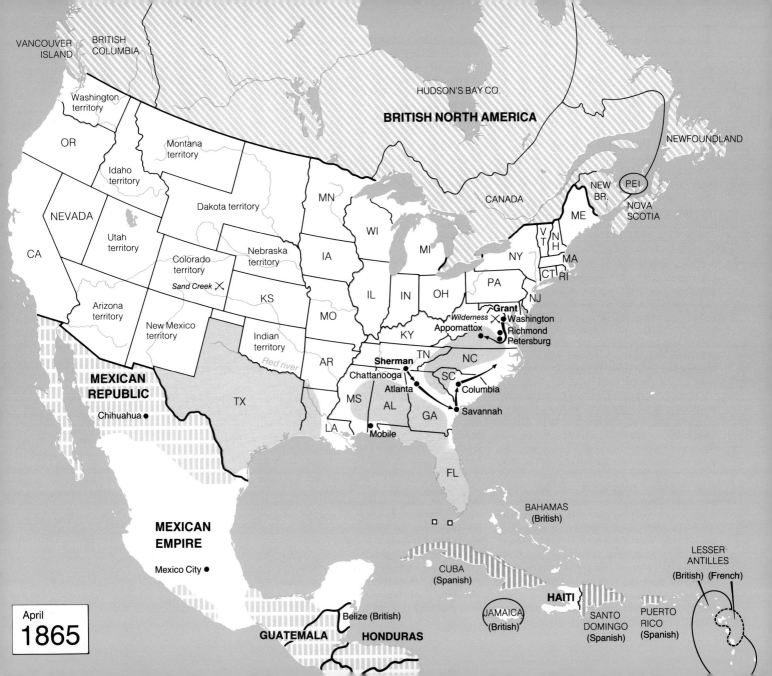

VANCOUVER ISLAND

BRITISH COLUMBIA

HUDSON'S BAY CO.

BRITISH NORTH AMERICA

NEWFOUNDLAND

CANADA

NEW BR.

PEI

NOVA SCOTIA

Washington territory

OR

Montana territory

Idaho territory

Dakota territory

MN

WI

MI

ME

VT NH

NY

MA

NEVADA

Utah territory

Nebraska territory

IA

PA

CT RI

NJ

CA

Arizona territory

Colorado territory

Sand Creek ✕

KS

MO

IL

IN

OH

KY

Grant

Wilderness ✕ Washington

Appomattox Richmond

Petersburg

New Mexico territory

Indian territory

Red river

AR

TN

NC

MEXICAN REPUBLIC

TX

Sherman

Chattanooga

Atlanta

MS

AL

GA

SC

Columbia

Savannah

Chihuahua ●

LA

Mobile

FL

MEXICAN EMPIRE

Mexico City ●

BAHAMAS (British)

CUBA (Spanish)

HAITI

LESSER ANTILLES (British) (French)

JAMAICA (British)

SANTO DOMINGO (Spanish)

PUERTO RICO (Spanish)

Belize (British)

GUATEMALA

HONDURAS

April 1865

The victory of the Union forces in the American Civil War determined the shape America was to take in the future. There would be no breakaway 'Confederate States of America'. The whole vast area between the Great Lakes in the north and the Rio Grande in the south, between the Atlantic Ocean in the east and the Pacific in the west, would be the domain of one nation. And by 1870 the shape of this nation had been determined not just in outline but in detail. To a surprising extent, the United States of 1870 was the United States of today. The external frontier achieved its final form when Alaska was purchased from the Russians in 1867 (for $1.7 million: the Russians, now the fur trade was past its best, were glad to sell) and though the number of states, at thirty-seven, was well below the present total of fifty, nearly all the rest were on the map in the form of territorial governments. The last important reshuffle had taken place in 1864 when the Wyoming territory was created. All that remained to be done was divide Dakota into North and South (as was done when the two were made States in 1889) and annex Hawaii – which is off our map anyway – in 1898.

Equally clear to anyone with a modicum of discernment was America's future status as a superpower. Demography alone was enough to ensure this. Every decade the population showed a substantial increase. In the 1860s, despite the loss of half a million men in the Civil War, numbers went up from something under 32 million to near enough 40 million. This was sufficient to put America ahead of every European state apart from Russia, where only seventy years earlier it would have ranked no better than eighth. Accelerating even faster than the population at large was the population in the cities. In 1800 the only city in the Americas with more than 100,000 inhabitants was Mexico City. By 1820 both New York and Philadelphia were of the same order of magnitude. By 1870 New York was in a class of its own – well over the million mark and, on a world scale, outranked only by London and Paris.

Industry was developing fast too. America might still lag behind Britain in the production of coal and iron, but she was ahead of everyone else, and would overtake Britain before the century was out. And in railroads she was already number one. The driving of the 'golden spike' at Ogden, Utah, in 1867, which celebrated the junction of the Central Pacific (running east from Sacramento, California) to the Union Pacific (running west from Omaha, Nebraska) was a moment worth savoring for many different reasons. It completed the transcontinental link that had been talked about for so long, it cemented the Union, now entering calm waters after the storms of the Civil War, it opened up vast new areas for development and it put America way ahead of everyone else in terms of track in use. By 1870 America had 53,000 miles of railroad in service, as against 16,000 in Britain and no more than 65,000 in all of Europe.

If the late 1860s were a period of relative calm in the United States, they were busy years for her neighbors to north and south. The British had been alarmed to hear that in the run-up to the Civil War some Americans had proposed invading Canada as an alternative to fighting among themselves. This off-hand attitude suggested that if British North America was to survive it needed a stronger political identity. Britain's answer was an act of Parliament which, in 1867, established the Dominion of Canada. The original components were Canada itself, in the form of the twin provinces of Ontario and Quebec, plus New Brunswick and Nova Scotia. In 1870 the Hudson's Bay Company transferred its charter lands to the Dominion in return for a handsome payment. A portion became the province of Manitoba; the major part was to be administered directly as the Northwest Territories. British Columbia joined the next year after getting a promise from the Dominion authorities to build a railroad across the Rockies within the next ten years. The government was slow to start this project but got the job finished almost on schedule, the Canadian Pacific finally opening for traffic in 1885. For laying the political foundation of the Dominion, credit is traditionally, and justly, given to its chief architect and first prime minister, John A. Macdonald.

The Mexican Republic discovered, in Benito Juarez, a founding father of equal stature. Juarez had twice been prevented from instituting the program of reform that Mexico so badly needed, first by home-grown *caudillos*, then by French intervention. The Juarist cause touched bottom in 1865 when Juarez was forced to abandon Chihuahua and take refuge in El Paso del Norte (since renamed Ciudad Juarez), a footstep from the American frontier. For a moment almost the entire country bowed to the authority of Maximilian, the puppet emperor the French had installed in Mexico City. Then the French took a second look at their Mexican adventure. The United States government had always disapproved of it and, now that the Civil War was over, was in a position to make its disapproval felt. The cost had already mounted beyond any possibility of recovery. Napoleon III, who knew when to curb his romantic inclinations, decided to pull out. He sent Maximilian an apologetic letter and ordered the French army to disengage, setting February 1867 as the embarkation date. At first Maximilian decided that he would have to go too, then he talked himself round, returned to Mexico City and led out what remained of his army against the Juaristas. While the last French troops were being ferried out to their ships in Vera Cruz harbor, Maximilian was in Queretero, trying to fight off encircling forces many times as strong as his own. In May he was forced to surrender, in June an implacable Juarez had him shot. Eighteen months earlier Maximilian had signed an order making the death penalty mandatory for captured rebels, and by that token his life was justly forfeited. All the same it makes a sad end to a silly story.

In the Caribbean the Spanish withdrew (for the second time) from the Dominican Republic.

BRITISH COLUMBIA

boundary of Dominion

DOMINION OF CANADA

Labrador (to Newfoundland)

Northwest territories

MANITOBA

boundary of Dominion

NEWFOUNDLAND

Washington territory

OR

Montana territory

Idaho territory

Dakota territory

MN

QUEBEC

PEI

NEW BR.

NOVA SCOTIA

acramento

Wyoming territory

WI

ONTARIO

ME

NV

Ogden

Utah territory

Colorado territory

NEBRASKA

IA

MI

VT NH

NY

MA

CA

Omaha

KS

IL

IN

OH

PA

CT RI

NJ

New York

Arizona territory

New Mexico territory

MO

Philadelphia

DE

WV

KY

VA

MD

Indian territory

AR

TN

NC

TX

MS

AL

GA

SC

LA

FL

REPUBLIC OF MEXICO

Queretero

BAHAMAS (British)

Mexico City

Vera Cruz

CUBA (Spanish)

LESSER ANTILLES

(British) (French)

December 1870

Belize (British)

GUATEMALA

HONDURAS

JAMAICA (British)

DOMINICAN REP.

HAITI

PUERTO RICO (Spanish)

EL SALVADOR

NICARAGUA

POSTSCRIPT: NORTH AMERICA TODAY

In essence the continental boundaries of Canada, the United States, Mexico and the Central American Republics are the same now as they were in 1870. Only one is still in dispute. Guatemala has a claim on Belize, whose independence, granted by the British in 1981, it refuses to recognize. This could cause a war one day, though not a very big one. The other frontiers in the area have been defined in a form acceptable to all parties.

As to constituent provinces, the most important developments are those in the Dominion of Canada. As already indicated on the previous page, the promise of a transcontinental rail connection induced British Columbia to join the Dominion in 1871. Prince Edward Island followed suit in 1873. Alberta and Saskatchewan, two new provinces created in 1905 from districts that had previously formed part of the Northwest Territories, were members from their first appearance. This left Newfoundland (with its dependency Labrador) as the only province outside the federation. Newfoundland retained its independence through the 1920s (when the present line between Labrador and Quebec province was defined) only to lose it in 1934 when the Great Depression bankrupted its government. After a recuperative period in which it was run by the British Colonial Office, Newfoundland finally voted itself into the Dominion in 1949.

The creation of Alberta and Saskatchewan and the progressive enlargement of Manitoba, Ontario and Quebec (in 1881, 1898 and 1912) brought all of Canada visible on this map into the provincial system. To the north of the western tier of provinces, in the area above 60°N, there remains a large slice of the Canadian mainland and an almost equally extensive collection of islands which have never known anything but territorial government. The Northwest Territories cover most of the area; the section nearest Alaska forms the separate Yukon Territory. The division dates from 1898, two years after the discovery of gold in the valley of the Klondike. This brought so many Americans into the Yukon that the Canadians felt they could well lose the area if they did not establish an effective administration for it.

In the United States the changes to note mostly concern the transformation of territories into states. Of the ten territories in existence in 1870 the first to be admitted to the Union was Colorado in 1876. The bumper year was 1889 when four states were made out of three territories: Washington, Montana and the two Dakotas. They were joined the next year by two more, Idaho and Wyoming. This should have reduced the number of territorial governments to four but a new one was set up that same year, Oklahoma. This consisted of the western half of the old Indian territory plus the strip of public land north of the Texas panhandle. The Indians had occupied less than half the land reserved for them and, as the years passed and the west filled up, white settlers pressed for permission to settle the vacant portion. In 1889 the first homesteaders were allowed in: by 1904 the entire Oklahoma territory had been opened up for white settlement. The final stage in the area's political evolution was taken in 1907 when the two territories were merged to form the State of Oklahoma.

As Utah had been made a state back in 1896, the admission of Oklahoma to the Union left only Arizona and New Mexico with territorial status. Both were made states in 1912. That completes the political evolution of the member states of the Union visible on this map. Off it lies Alaska, made a territory in 1912 and a state in 1958, and Hawaii, annexed in 1898 and made a state in 1959.

The Caribbean has seen a great many changes. It now contains eleven sovereign states as against two, Haiti and the Dominican Republic, in 1870. The most important of the newcomers is undoubtedly Cuba which, along with Puerto Rico, was freed from Spanish rule as a result of the Spanish–American war of 1898. For the next half century and more Cuba remained in America's orbit: then in 1959 it was taken over by a group of Marxist rebels headed by Fidel Castro. He made the country a member of the Soviet bloc, a transformation which, with conditions and after some interventions that proved nail-biting occasions for all concerned, the United States has shown itself prepared to accept.

The other ex-Spanish island, Puerto Rico, passed to the United States as a dependent territory, a status in which it has continued, by its own wish, ever since. Most of the neighboring Virgin Islands are also American possessions: they were purchased from Denmark for $25 million in 1917. The few Virgin Islands that are not American are British, as are several other small islands in the neighborhood.

The British originally intended to put all their islands in the Caribbean into an umbrella organization called the West Indies Federation. This would have enabled them to unload responsibility for the smaller islands on the larger ones, notably Jamaica. The Jamaicans, however, were not having it and, in 1958, voted themselves out of the scheme. Since then the British have conferred independence on such of the islands as could sustain it, while retaining responsibility for the rest. The end result is that the United Nations has been enriched by no less than ten island governments, eight on the map (the Bahamas, Jamaica, Antigua-Barbuda, St Kitts-Nevis, Dominica, St Lucia, Barbados and St Vincent) and two just off it (Grenada and Trinidad-Tobago). That still leaves half a dozen islands under the rule of the British Colonial Office, notably the Turks and Caicos (the easternmost members of the Bahamas), the Caymans, some small islands in the Windward group (not shown) and, way off to the north, Bermuda. The Dutch and French also have some dependencies in the Windwards (not shown either). The main French islands in the Caribbean, Guadeloupe and Martinique, have been made into overseas departments of France.

ADDITIONAL NOTES

1628

1 At the time of the capture of the Silver Fleet the Spanish were still trying to recover from an earlier disaster, the loss of two treasure ships in a storm in 1622. The *Margarita* and the *Atocha* set out from Havana at the wrong time of year, got caught in a hurricane and were swept on to the Florida keys. The Spanish found the *Margarita* and in 1626–8 managed to salvage most of her cargo, but had no luck in their search for the *Atocha*. Neither did anyone else until 1985 when a team of professional underwater explorers located the wreck. Their success came at the end of a long and expensive search for which it is safe to presume they will be handsomely rewarded.

1702

1 Some French authorities assert that La Salle discovered the upper reaches of the Ohio during a journey he made to the south of Lake Erie in 1671. However, there is no evidence that he got so far and the claim is now discounted. In truth La Salle was not interested in exploration for its own sake and does not seem to have visited even the most spectacular discovery made by any of his expeditions, Niagara Falls. The credit for this belongs to Father Hennepin, a missionary who accompanied La Salle through the Great Lakes in 1678–9 and traced the sound of the Falls, which was audible at the base camp on Lake Erie, to its source. His account of the Falls, published in Europe in 1683, created a great stir, not least because he estimated their height at 500 feet, a threefold improvement on the true figure of 167 feet.

2 Two colonial governments that were not re-established were Plymouth and Maine: both were incorporated in Massachusetts by the charter of 1691. To the disappointment of Massachusetts, the charter did not include jurisdiction over New Hampshire, whose separate identity was confirmed by the Crown the next year.

3. The Indian war of 1675–6 is known as King Philip's War after the leading figure on the Indian side, who was given this name by the colonists. His real name was Metacomet. The war of 1689–98 is called King William's War in American history books (after the reigning English King, William III) while in Europe it is referred to as the War of the League of Augsburg.

4 During the second half of the seventeenth century, English loggers began operating in the forests along the Mexican and Caribbean coasts of Yucatan; by 1700 they had established permanent camps in Campeche Bay and Belize. The Spaniards were determined to drive them out and succeeded as regards the Campeche group in 1717.

1750

1 Port Royal, renamed Annapolis by the British, retained its capital status until Halifax was founded in 1749.

By the terms of the Treaty of Utrecht the British also got the French half of St Kitts in the Caribbean and, something that they probably considered more important than all their other gains, the right to sell up to 4,800 slaves a year in the Spanish colonial market.

An aspect of Queen Anne's War that deserves a few lines is the continuing story of raid and counter-raid across the divide between New France on the one hand and New York and New England on the other. The French maintained their advantage in this. Their allies, the Abnaki, proved unexpectedly active, while their enemies, the Iroquois, were nursing such heavy casualties from the previous round of fighting that they proved reluctant combatants. As a result, the colonization of northern New York, New Hampshire and Maine suffered a severe set-back.

POPULATION IN 1750

1 Most of those who did survive were members of the Iroquois Confederacy, the only social unit with the cohesion to protect its members from piecemeal destruction. Indeed the Iroquois actually increased in numbers during the seventeenth and early eighteenth centuries. This was partly because when they defeated an enemy tribe they took over its women and children, and partly because their prestige stood so high that some tribes joined them voluntarily. The most famous instance of this occurred in 1712 when the Tuscarora of North Carolina, after a sharp defeat at the hands of the local colonists, migrated north and applied to join the confederacy. The request was granted in 1722, an event which transformed the Five Nations of the original union into Six.

DECEMBER 1796

1 Cape Breton Island was given provincial status at the same time as New Brunswick. It was to lose this, and be reabsorbed into Nova Scotia, in 1820.

2 Washington left the Presidency before Washington city, the new Federal capital, was ready for occupation. The move was made in 1800 when the government was transferred there from Philadelphia by his successor, John Adams.

3 The political position on St Domingue was curious. A slave revolt in 1791 destroyed the plantation system and decimated the white population. Subsequently most of the surviving whites fled the country. However, the various black and mulatto bands that emerged in the course of the struggle were not as yet ready to assume power and continued to recognize the authority, albeit nominal, of the French government. The French felt they could make something of this situation and in 1795 persuaded Spain to cede them the eastern half of the island.

4 In the north-west, note the exploration of the Strait of Juan de Fuca and its various ramifications. Whether or not Juan de Fuca had ever set eyes on it, it was entered for sure by a British vessel passing along the coast in 1787. Five years later both the Spanish and the British were actively exploring the area, the British being represented by one of Cook's ablest lieutenants, George Vancouver. These maritime expeditions were complemented by the epic overland journey of Alexander MacKenzie, on behalf of the North-West Fur Company, across the Rockies to the Pacific coast. This is the first continental crossing we know of anywhere north of the Rio Grande. The track, unfortunately, lies at the upper margin of our map.

The British forced the Spanish to abandon their claims to the north-west by insisting on the principle that sovereignty extended only as far as settlement. This left the area open to all comers, among them the Americans who, while not contributing much to its exploration in this opening phase, did investigate and name one of its major features, the Columbia River.

JULY 1822

1 The period 1806–22 saw the admission of seven new states to the Union, increasing the total from seventeen to twenty-four. The Orleans territory became the State of Louisiana in 1812 and the Mississippi territory was divided between the States of Mississipi (1817) and Alabama (1819). Each of these three got a slice of what had previously been Spanish west Florida. In the north-west, Indiana achieved statehood in 1816 and Illinois in 1818. Finally, Maine, previously a district of Massachusetts, and Missouri, part of the Louisiana Purchase, were admitted to the Union as a result of the legislative compromise of 1820 (for which see p. 72).

2 Russians engaged in the hunt for sea otters established a temporary base just north of San Francisco in 1809, moved to a new site (Rossiya or 'Fort Ross') three years later and stayed there till the sea otter was near exterminated, a matter of some twenty-five years. The post had no political significance: in 1824–5, in parallel treaties with the United States and Britain, Russia renounced any interest in the coast south of 54° 40′.

Labrador, the north coast of the Gulf of St Lawrence and the island of Anacosti were placed under the jurisdiction of Newfoundland in 1809. Newfoundland has retained control over Labrador ever since, but the Gulf coast and Anacosti were recovered by Quebec in 1825.

3 Other points to notice on this map are the opening of the Santa Fe trail to New Mexico in 1821 and the conquest of Spanish Santo Domingo by Haiti's new strong man, General Jean-Pierre Boyers.

Index

This is an index to the text, not the maps. For geographical locations try the map opposite the first entry in the index. This will only work for American names, of course, and not always for them: Alaska and Panama, for example, lie outside the area covered by the base map.